W9-BUF-893

GUYS AND A WHOLE LOT MORE

Advice for Teen Girls on Almost Everything!

Susie Shellenberger

Fleming H. Revell
A Division of Baker Book House Co
Grand Rapids, Michigan 49516

© 1994 by Susie Shellenberger

Published by Fleming H. Revell
a division of Baker Book House Company
P.O. Box 6287, Grand Rapids, MI 49516-6287

Printed in the United States of America

All rights reserved. No part of this publication may be reproduced, stored in a retrieval system, or transmitted in any form or by any means—electronic, mechanical, photocopy, recording, or any other—without the prior written permission of the publisher. The only exception is brief quotations in printed reviews.

Library of Congress Cataloging-in-Publication Data

Shellenberger, Susie.
    Guys and a whole lot more : advice for teen girls on almost everything! / Susie Shellenberger.
    p. cm.
    ISBN 0-8007-5532-4
    1. Teenage girls—Religious life. 2. Christian life—Juvenile literature. 3. Teenage girls—Conduct of life. I. Title.
    BV4551.2.S48 1994
    248.8'33 — dc20   94-11459

Unless otherwise indicated, Scripture quotations are taken from *The Living Bible,* copyright © 1971 by Tyndale House Publishers, Wheaton, Illinois. Used by permission.

Some of these questions first appeared in *Brio* magazine, published by Focus on the Family.

Dedicated to ...

My grandma, Mrs. Grace Shellenberger. As I write these words, you're about to celebrate your 100th birthday. For thirty-seven out of those one hundred years I have seen Jesus in your life. Thank you for the positive, godly heritage you have given me. I love you.

Special acknowledgment to ...

Gaye Marston. Thanks for your professional insight. I value your advice and am grateful for your friendship. You are one of my very favorite people to laugh with.

And for my two best friends ...

Dr. and Mrs. Elmer B. Shellenberger. You never got tired of my curiosity but allowed me the freedom to ask a million questions. If I could have created my own parents, I would have asked God for *you*.

GUYS
AND A
WHOLE LOT MORE

Reasons I'm going to read this book:

a. It was a gift and I feel like I *have* to.
b. I want to know more about guys.
c. Our teacher said we have to have *something* to read during free time.
d. I'm interested in what other girls my age are dealing with.
e. It's past midnight and McDonald's is closed and I'm bored and there's nothing good on TV and I can't go to sleep, so hey, I might as well.
f. I want to write a book myself someday, and I figured I'd check out what this one has to say.
g. I have a few questions about my body.
h. I'm sick of *Saved by the Bell* reruns.
i. I don't wanna do my homework.
j. I'm on a bus to camp and don't want to sing "100 Bottles of Coke on the Wall" with everyone else.
k. It's too hot to be outside.
l. It's too cold to be outside.
m. I've read some of Susie's other books and liked them.
n. If I'm not reading something, Mom will ask me to make dinner, unload the dishwasher, or clean my room.
o. Some of my friends are going through a superhard time and I wanna know how to help them better.

p. I'm bedridden. Too sick to go to school but not sick enough to sleep all the time. I gotta do *something*.

q. I want some advice on improving my self-esteem.

r. My youth minister said I'd like it.

s. I ask my Sunday school teacher too many questions, so she gave me this. She said I'd find most of the answers in here.

t. It's either this or practice the piano.

u. I really want to know more about how to strengthen my relationship with Christ.

v. I've been abused and don't want to tell anyone.

w. I want to know how to get a guy to notice me.

x. I'm curious to see if my city or state is listed in here somewhere.

y. I don't understand why my friend is so depressed.

z. I wanna know what Susie has to say to someone who wants to buy a snake.

Whatever your reasons for reading this, I want to remind you that a question/answer book always reflects the opinions and beliefs of its author. Therefore, I'm sharing with you what *I* think based on my personal understanding of God's Word. Let me know what you think, okay? You can write me at the address listed in the back of the book.

Susie

STUFF THAT'S IN THIS BOOK

1

WHAT'S GOING ON WITH MY BODY?

I DON'T HAVE PERIODS. I HAVE EXCLAMATION POINTS!

Dear Susie:

I have superbad cramps during my period. Sometimes they're so bad I have to miss school. What can I do?

Charlotte,
North Carolina

First, try an over-the-counter painkiller that contains ibuprofen.

Sometimes *light* exercise helps. A short walk, for instance, will help your muscles relax—which will cause the cramps to ease a bit.

You didn't mention the doctor . . . but he or she could prescribe something stronger than what we've already talked about. If there's a waiting list for an appointment, ask your mom to call the nurse. She can probably get a prescription from your doctor over the phone. I've done this several times.

Dear Susie:

I'm fourteen years old and very short for my age. I hate it when people tease me because of my size. I feel like I'm six years old. How do I make them realize that I'm not a little girl?

Sacramento, California

I'm short too! I don't mind, though, because I learned a long time ago that one of the reasons teens tease each other is because it usually evokes a response from the one being teased. When it's no longer fun, the teasing usually stops.

My suggestion? Laugh along with those who are teasing you; even make a joke out of it yourself.

It's my guess that when your "tormentors" realize it no longer bothers you, they'll give it up.

You ask, "How do I make them realize that I'm not a little girl?" A little girl gets upset easily (and shows it) when others tease her. Maturity, however, laughs in the face of opposition.

I'd like to share a letter with you that I received recently.

Dear Susie:

I'm fifteen years old and only three feet, ten inches tall. I am an achondroplasia dwarf (or a little person). It's hard being so short, but I also have fun joking about myself.

At my eighth-grade graduation, I told a friend, "Stop wearing heels—you make me look shorter!" We both laughed.

I call myself "Shrimp Cocktail" and "Short Stuff." It may sound like I don't mind being a dwarf—but I actually hate it. I went through a time of being angry at God. It's frustrating to have people constantly stare at me and

12

point. But you know what? God has a purpose in allowing me to be a dwarf. He created me just the way I am—special and unique.

Now that I've made peace in trusting HIM with my feelings of anger and confusion, I can laugh. It not only helps me, but it makes those around me feel more at ease also.

Dear Susie:

One of my friends said that when you have your period, it stops when you get in the water. My other friend said she got her period in the bathtub. Which is true?

Houston, Texas

Getting in and out of the water has no effect on your period.

Dear Susie:

My best friend is overweight. I feel embarrassed when she wears very tight jeans or really pigs out in a group. I told her I thought she should lose weight. What else can I do?

Uniontown, Ohio

I appreciate your concern for your friend, but I have to ask if it's really concern for *her,* or simply what people will think of *you* knowing she's your best friend?

People who are overweight know it. They don't need someone else to call it to their attention. It's my guess that your friend feels bad enough already. She probably thinks and worries about her weight more than you can imagine. Many times when someone approaches an overweight person about how much they weigh, it drives them to eat more.

My suggestion? Don't just *tell* her you care, *show* her. Why not suggest you *both* take an aerobics class to-

13

gether? The fact that you're offering to be involved also takes the attention off her and will keep her from feeling pressured by you.

Dear Susie:

I'm fifteen and I still don't wear a bra. My mom thinks I need to, but I don't *want* to wear one. I couldn't stand having an uncomfortable tightness around me and don't think we should be harnessed like that. We're women, not horses! I want to be free.

Preston, Washington

No one wants to wear something uncomfortable, but I think you can find a bra that fits great and feels good to have on. The advantage of wearing a bra eliminates that "naked" look under a blouse or sweater. And it offers important support so your tissue doesn't break down, making your breasts sag later. Did you know you can buy a cotton/knit T-shirt-type bra? They don't feel binding, have no padding, yet offer some support. Ask for one of these, and just try it on. You might be surprised.

Dear Susie:

About a year ago I got a perm. Bad idea! I didn't get any wave, body, or curl. All I got was LOTS of split ends and poofiness! Is there any kind of shampoo or conditioner I can use to help heal my hair? I don't want to cut it short because it grows really slow. And I don't want to spend a lot of money.

Louisville, Kentucky

Sounds like your perm was overprocessed. Sometimes a beautician will do a cut on someone else while you're processing, and the result is often that the solution is left on too long. The damage is not noticeable at first because when your hair is wet it's curly, but after drying, you notice how fuzzy it is.

First, let's talk about what *not* to do. Don't get another perm—that would just add more damage to the damage you already have. And don't overblow-dry it; that simply exagger-ates the problem.

DO get a leave-in conditioner. Put a little in the palm of your hand, then work it through your hair with your fingers and leave it in. Why use a leave-in conditioner? Because the ordinary kind most people use after shampooing just coats the outside of the hair—it's kind of like waxing your head. A leave-in conditioner actually gets into the hair shaft and conditions from the inside out.

DO continue to trim your hair. Just letting it grow out will prolong the fuzzy look. By getting it trimmed every four to six weeks, you're consistently getting rid of the dead ends.

Dear Susie:

Help! I have bird legs. What's the best way to build up muscles in my calves? Any particular exercise that would really help?

Pittsburgh,
Pennsylvania

Try this calf-crunchie to tone up your calves and shins: Grab the edge of a chair or countertop. Lift up on your toes as high as you can. Now slowly lower your heels back down to the floor. For an extra workout, balance the front half of your feet on the edge of a step. Lower yourself as far down as you can. Now, push up as high as you can. Keep doing it . . . repeat ten times.

Dear Susie:

I recently moved from Arizona to San Diego. I'm having a hard time adjusting in my new school. I only have one real friend, and I'm much more shy than normal kids my age.

Also, I swim regularly and my hair often has a green tint to it. I get teased all the time about my hair and my

16

looks. I'm beyond unpopular. We have year-round school and I hate it! I don't really get a chance to start over. Please help me!

San Diego, California

I know moving, living in new surroundings, and going to a new school are all BIG adjustments, but guess what? You're not alone! Jesus goes *with* you. He promised *never* to leave you or abandon you. He feels the loneliness, fear, and apprehension with you. He also wants to help you *through* it!

Begin each day by praying, "Lord, teach me that you love me today." Then actively look for his signs throughout the day. They may be big or little signs, but in some way he'll remind you how much he loves you. Someone you don't know very well might smile at you. As soon as that happens, breathe a word of thanks to God for proof that he cares.

You might summon the courage to sit with a few kids at lunch whom you don't know very well. Super! Thank God for giving you the courage to make that step. If you ask him, he'll bombard you with love in a bazillion surprises throughout your day.

About starting over; could it be that God wants to be your strength *within* your hard times, instead of simply giving you the easy way out?

And about the green tint to your hair; the only thing that will cut through the chlorine buildup is a swimmer's shampoo. They're available at beauty supply stores (and maybe in a few grocery stores). The key, though, is using it immediately after swimming.

The drier your hair gets, the more porous it becomes— meaning the chlorine penetrates and sticks to your hair more. It's sort of a catch-22. The more you swim, the drier your hair becomes; and the drier your hair gets, the more visible the chlorine will be. There *is* some good

17

news, though! Swimming is one of the best things you can do to get in shape. I encourage you to continue your great fitness program even though you're not completely satisfied with your hair.

Dear Susie:

I'm thirteen years old and have had my period for almost a year, but I have never used a tampon. I would like to know how because I *hate* using pads. My mom and my friends are convinced that tampons are much better and more comfortable than even the thinnest pad.

I have tried to insert a tampon several times, but it hurts and I just can't make it fit right. Any suggestions on how I can learn this?

Also, I've never gone to a gynecologist. When do you suggest I should start going?

Hayden Lake, Idaho

If your mom is saying tampons are the answer, why not talk with her about the trouble you're having? You've already talked about them to *some* degree, so I'm guessing it wouldn't be too uncomfortable to ask her about them the next time she mentions how wonderful they are. Have the instructions in the box been clear? You could probably ask your mom about this too.

The key, though, is being patient and relaxed. Try taking a warm bath (warm water has a relaxing effect on the body), and after you get out, try again.

Also, make sure you're using the thinnest tampon you can find. Tampax has a "slender" size—buy some of those. If you're still having trouble, apply a small amount of a water-based lubricant to the end of the tampon before you insert it (one well-known brand is K-Y Jelly). You *don't* want to use hand or body lotions—they may cause irritation or infection.

If you keep trying on and off for a year and still can't insert one, you might want to ask your doctor about it. And when should you go to a gynecologist? Unless you're having a specific female problem, you probably don't need your first Pap smear or pelvic exam until you're twenty-one.

Dear Susie:

I've heard that if you wear a bra to bed your breasts won't grow. Is this true?

Simi Valley, California

I've never heard this! I have heard, though, that the Chinese used to tightly wrap their daughter's feet in cloths so they would have small feet as adults. (I guess it was a sign of beauty to have small feet.)

I suppose if someone bound their chest extremely tight, it could stunt some growth. But wearing a bra to bed is a far cry from being tightly bound. No, I don't think sleeping with a bra on will keep your breasts from growing.

Dear Susie:

I'm fourteen years old and I think I just had my first period, but I'm not sure. I have no underarm hair, only a little pubic hair, and my breasts aren't that big.

My mom started her period when she was nineteen, and my older sister started when she was fifteen.

During the night I felt nothing, but when I woke up there was a lot of brown in my underwear. After that night nothing has happened. What should I do? Should I be expecting more, or is there some kind of delay I don't know about?

Gallatin, Tennessee

Yes, you've had the beginnings of your first period. And yes, more is coming. It will probably happen next month, but since there's no way to know *exactly* when, it's a good idea to be prepared. Carry a pad or tampon in your purse just in case it happens when you're away from home.

Dear Susie:

What's the best way to get a tan without going to a salon?

Omaha, Nebraska

There are several quick-tanning lotions that don't require being in the sun to get that golden look. The less expensive ones are available at your local drugstore; others can be purchased for a few dollars more from a cosmetics counter in any shopping mall.

Caution: Beware of inexpensive tanning lotions that promise the golden-goddess look in ten minutes. That's almost a surefire promise to turn you orange or even rust-colored. Also, if it colors quickly, it probably comes off quickly.

Dear Susie:

Is it true that if you put lemon juice on your hair and sit in the sun that it acts as a bleach?

Parkersburg, West Virginia

You got it. In fact, *I* used lemon juice a few years ago. It really does lighten your hair (unless you have black hair). It stays in for a couple of weeks, depending on how much you put on and how often you stay in the sun.

Though it works as a lightener, I'm not sure it's really that good for your hair.

Dear Susie:

How old should you be when you start wearing makeup?

Orlando, Florida

You probably won't like this, but I think your parents are going to have to answer that one. A lot of it depends on personal maturity. Some thirteen-year-olds are more mature than some sixteen-year-olds. Since I don't know you or your parents' convictions, I suggest you talk with your mom.

One other thought, makeup should be used to *enhance* your natural beauty. It won't give you something you don't have. In other words, don't expect to become someone else when you start wearing it; rather, use it to highlight the great aspects that already make you uniquely beautiful.

Dear Susie:

I'm frustrated! I'm going through all the signs of puberty (irritability, confusion, aches, zits), but nothing's happening. I'm sick of the suspense. Got any advice?

South Burl, Utah

There's absolutely nothing you can do to speed the process. Most girls will begin their period sometime between the ages of ten and fifteen. But it's okay if you're earlier or later than that. Each person is God's unique and wonderful creation.

When others are "bragging" about their periods, just smile and know your time will come—and be grateful that you're not cramping like they probably are.

Dear Susie:

I'm eleven years old and have noticed a clear discharge on my underwear. Is this normal?

Moundridge, Kansas

This is often a premenstrual sign. You may be getting your first period in the next couple of months. Talk with your mom about using pads or tampons.

21

Dear Susie:

I've had my period for three years, and I'm *still* not regular. Could something be wrong?

Peoria, Illinois

It's not unusual for girls to be irregular for the first few years, but how irregular are we talking about? If you're a few days early or late that's one thing . . . but if you're having a period every other week or only one a year, that's a different matter.

If you're *very* irregular, consider seeing your family doctor.

Dear Susie:

I'm thirteen years old and have a very flat chest. Are there any exercises I can do to enlarge my breasts?

Houston, Texas

Breast size is determined more by heredity than anything else. Many women believe that working out with weights will increase their bust size, but our breasts are made up of fatty tissue, not muscle. Lifting or pressing weights won't enlarge fatty tissue. It will, however, make your breasts more toned and defined.

Dear Susie:

I'm sixteen years old and have been anorexic since I was twelve. I'm better now but still have a lot of stuff to work through. I have a very low self-esteem and have considered suicide.

I'd really like to talk with a female Christian counselor, but I live in a small town and this simply isn't available. I won't talk to my parents about it because they'd say it costs too much, and I don't trust them. I don't feel comfortable sharing this with our pastor either. I feel totally alone in this.

Bozeman, Montana

Most people with an eating disorder *do* feel all alone—
as though absolutely no one in the world understands.
But there *are* people who understand, and there are
people who can help.

The problem is about more than food or weight . . . it's
what's going on *underneath* your weight problem. What
is that? I don't know. And you probably don't know either.
That's why you need someone else who's knowledgeable
about eating disorders to guide you through this.

And I agree with you, I think a female Christian counselor would be your best choice. Your parents may be
right about the cost; but can you see this as something
so worth dealing with that you'd be willing to keep asking them again and again and again about shelling out
some money for your healing?

I understand that you don't want to talk with them
about getting help. But I'll bet if you had a life-threaten-
ing illness they would help you get the needed treatment.
How important is it to you that you get well?

Since there is not a Christian counselor in your town,
try to locate one in the next closest town. Meanwhile,
get some books on eating disorders from your local library. The suggested reading list at the back of the book
has some titles you might look for. Though these will not
help you uncover specifically what problems are going
on underneath your weight problem, they may provide
some needed insight.

Dear Susie:

I have heard that you lose weight when you're
depressed. I'm not depressed but I have lost a lot of
weight in the past month. Is this normal?

McAllen, Texas

You're partly right. *Some* people who are depressed
lose weight. But guess what? Others tend to gain weight
when depressed. Other signs of depression are irri-

tability, sadness, anxiety, restlessness, and a feeling of worthlessness. Many girls have trouble sleeping. Others oversleep. Loss of energy, getting tired easily, losing interest in hobbies, and withdrawing from people are other signs.

You say you've lost a lot of weight, but what's a lot? If you've dropped five to seven pounds, I'd be tempted to say your body is experiencing some of the many physical changes that puberty brings. If you've lost more than that, I suggest you talk to your parents about making an appointment with your family doctor.

Dear Susie:

My breasts are just beginning to develop. I'm really embarrassed because one is larger than the other. What's wrong with me?

Colorado Springs, Colorado

Relax. You're completely normal! *Every* woman's breasts are slightly different in size—just like your feet. One is just a *little bit* bigger than the other one.

When our breasts first begin to develop, they don't grow at the same rate. Sometimes it's more noticeable than at other times, but you're normal. They're both going to turn out okay. I promise.

GUY BREAK!

Dear Susie:

I really like this guy at church. My problem is that my parents don't like him at all. See, he has long hair and plays the drums. His parents are kind of wild. He's already asked me out, and I want to say yes. But how do I break it to my folks?

Forest Park, Ohio

When your parents say no to something, it's not because they're working overtime to spoil your fun, but rather because of their love for you. They're obviously seeing some things you're not seeing (due to the fact that your emotions are stronger than your logic right now).

I think you already know the answer. Obey your folks. Later, you'll be glad you did. I promise.

Dear Susie:

How can I help my friend over the pain of finding out that the boy she likes has his eyes on someone else?

Mellette, South Dakota

There's absolutely nothing you can do to make this news painless. It will hurt! And it'll hurt *big*. So should you tell her? Well, it doesn't sound like they're dating. Your letter describes her as being in the "liking him" stage. If they were dating each other and he was cheating on her, I think it would be important to share this information—but only if you were absolutely sure, beyond all doubt—that it was true. Since they're not exactly in a relationship with each other, he certainly has the right to like any girl he chooses. I'd refrain from telling her. She'll find out soon enough. And when she does, be there for her.

2

SOMETIMES I FEEL PRESSURE TO DO WHAT EVERYONE ELSE IS DOING

Dear Susie:

A lot of my friends like to watch horror movies—you know, your basic *Freddy* or *Friday the 13th* stuff. My mom says they'll give me nightmares. Even if they wouldn't, I think they're garbage anyway.

I haven't been in a situation where I've had to choose to stay or leave, but if I am, what should I do without feeling like an outcast?

Springville, New York

I'm proud of you! You're being smart by choosing not to view that stuff. Ever heard of the phrase "garbage in/garbage out"? Whatever we put into our minds will eventually come out in our lifestyles. Sneak a peak at what Jesus tells us in Mark 7:21–23: "For from within, out of men's hearts, come evil thoughts of lust, theft, murder, adultery, wanting what belongs to others, wickedness, deceit, lewdness, envy, slander, pride, and all other folly. All these vile things come from within;

they are what pollute you and make you unfit for God." That's pretty much what you're going to see by watching horror flicks, isn't it?

How can you keep from feeling like an outcast by not joining the crowd? Well, you probably *will* feel like an outcast. To be honest, most of your friends won't understand why you choose not to watch those movies.

Jesus never promised it would be easy to do the right thing, but he *did* promise to give us the strength to do it. "It is quite true that the way to live a godly life is not an easy matter. But the answer lies in Christ" (1 Tim. 3:16a).

So how about suggesting an alternate plan to your circle of movie mates? Explain the situation to your parents and ask if you can initiate a "plan B" at your house with some fun classics like *Anne of Green Gables, The Parent Trap,* or *The Sound of Music.*

Dear Susie:

I used to live in New York but moved to New Jersey over a year ago. Though I lived in a dangerous part of NYC, the kids weren't bad. At my new school, however, it's completely different.

I've met kids here who have lost their virginity and have been smoking since the fifth grade. (I'm in the ninth grade now.) My old classmates hadn't even started dating yet. They didn't wear makeup very often either. But at my new school all the girls wear makeup.

I can't wear makeup because my church feels it's wrong. What can I do to fit in without going against my beliefs and having to change my personality?

Bergenfield, New Jersey

Moving from one school/city/state is tough because it means *change.* And change always means *adjustment.* Some changes are easier than others. I'm sorry this has been such a difficult one.

I'm proud of you, though, for expressing your desire to fit in *without changing.* All of us want to be accepted. The danger comes when we choose to compromise in order to fit in.

How can you be more accepted? It's almost impossible to turn down love. So try pouring it on those around you. How? Display a gentle personality and like *yourself* (so you can truly like others). Make some cookies or brownies and place little notes of kindness on each one as you deliver them to different lockers.

Kindness, laughter, and personality go a lot further than makeup, fashion, and style. I want to encourage you to keep your standards high. Check out Romans 12:1–2 for some great advice on staying above the crowd, and take comfort in the fact that Jesus walks through the tough times *with* you.

Dear Susie:

My friend is having a slumber party and she wants to use a Ouija board. What does a Ouija board really do? How should I respond if I'm in a situation where I'm asked to play with one?

Torrance, California

A Ouija board is often used at séances, gatherings in which people sit in a circle and try to communicate with loved ones who are dead. A Ouija board is a flat board with the alphabet written on it. It also comes with a plastic triangle (about the size of your palm). The object of the game is to place your fingers lightly on the triangle while asking the board a question. Then, supposedly, the triangle moves—of its own power, not yours—to various letters across the board to spell out an answer.

What makes the triangle move? Sometimes the tension from the hands of the participants; sometimes evil spirits. Yep, that's it—bottom line—I believe Ouija boards are satanic. So are séances (see Deut. 18:9–14).

The Bible tells us to go to God for our source of direction. If we want answers, why not go to the Creator of life itself? Check out what James 1:5 says: "If you want to know what God wants you to do, ask him, and he will gladly tell you, for he is always ready to give a bountiful supply of wisdom to all who ask him; he will not resent it."

I've talked with people who got messed up in satanic cults, and guess what? They all say the same thing: it started with simple games like séances, Ouija boards, and horoscopes.

How should you respond if you're being pressured to play with one? LEAVE! And stay as far away from Ouija boards as possible!

Dear Susie:

I'm in the eighth grade, and this is my first year in a public school. It's been a pretty tough adjustment. There's one girl in particular who's really giving me a hard time. She recently asked me if I was a virgin. I told her I was, and now she's spreading it around and the boys are making fun of me.

Isn't there something I can say that would make them shut up?

Jacksonville, Florida

I'm sorry you're having such a rough time, but I'm really proud of you for maintaining high morals. God's Word is pretty clear on the subject of premarital sex. He wants us to wait till marriage for some good reasons.

To take the fun out of life?

No, to PROTECT us! There are *more than* fifty sexually transmitted diseases . . . and many have absolutely no cure. Your sexually active classmates may be bragging about "safe sex" now, but will they still be bragging in a few years? Here's the truth: There IS no safe sex outside of marriage!

Josh McDowell once told the story of a girl (like you) who was constantly being teased by her schoolmates because of her virginity. One day she had enough and spoke up at the lunch table.

"At any moment I can choose to become like any one of you. But none of you can *ever* become like me. You've lost it forever."

Guess what? They never teased her again.

Keep it up: your chin, your standards, your walk with God.

Dear Susie:

There are some teens in my youth group whom I really admire spiritually. But I also know that they'd kiss someone they hardly knew if they played "spin the bottle," "seven minutes in the closet," or other similar games.

Is this okay with God as long as you aren't involved with someone else?

Janesville, Wisconsin

There's nothing wrong with wanting to kiss a guy. Those are natural feelings that God created in you. But kissing is only okay in the right context.

I believe it's wrong to kiss just to be kissing. I also believe it's wrong to kiss a guy because you feel obligated to. (For instance, at the end of a date many girls think, *Well, he spent a lot of money on me tonight; guess I better kiss him.)*

So when is it okay to kiss a guy? When you're involved in a genuine, loving, mature relationship and it actually means something. Kissing someone as a result of "spin the bottle" or any other pressure-filled game hardly meets any of those requirements.

Sorry, but the friends you look up to are simply yielding to peer pressure. Don't make the same mistake.

Dear Susie:

I go to a public school, and most of the students swear. Sometimes I'm tempted to join in with them, but so far I haven't. In fact, I've *never* sworn before. I believe it's wrong . . . but now I'm beginning to question this belief. Does it really matter how I speak as long as I've asked God to save me? Or should I not swear, period?

Conway, Arkansas

It matters. Ephesians 5:1 tells us to be imitators of God. Would HE swear? Matthew 5:13–16 tells us we're to be lights to those around us. Does swearing help someone else see God in your life?

Swearing with God's name is such a big deal to him that he made it a part of the Ten Commandments (see Exod. 20:7). Again, *it matters.* Your non-Christian friends don't need to see how much you have in common with them; they need to see the difference Christ makes in your life!

Let's sneak a peak at what Ephesians 4:29 says: "Don't use bad language. Say only what is good and helpful to those you are talking to, and what will give them a blessing."

Wow. That sums it up, doesn't it? I realize it's tough. I used to teach in a public high school. Foul language permeated the hallways, cafeteria, and even the classrooms. But God has a higher calling on your life. And in his strength you can rise above the mediocrity around you.

Dear Susie:

I recently went to church camp for a week, and the speaker challenged us to bring our Bibles to school. My mom always told me not to, because I'm not ready for the criticism I'll get at my public school. Now she says it's my decision. What should I do?

Gilbertsville, Pennsylvania

I used to be a speech and drama teacher in a public high school, and I always admired kids who brought their Bibles to school. It showed me they weren't just being Christians on Sundays—when it was easy—but during the week, in the "blackboard jungle" where things sometimes get tense.

Jesus tells us that if we'll acknowledge him on earth, he'll acknowledge us to his Father. He wants us to take a stand, share our beliefs, and speak out for him.

It's also important, though, that you obey the class rules and use common sense. If your teacher has asked everyone to read chapter seven in your textbook, it's not the right time to bring out your Bible. Or if you're supposed to be writing an essay, don't read your Bible instead. Do what you're assigned. Jesus told his disciples to obey the laws of the land and to pay their taxes.

I encourage you to carry your Bible. Yeah, you may get reamed on by a few classmates, but try to look past that and realize that God will impact others through you.

Dear Susie:

How can I tell when a guy is really being sincere? I talk to this guy on the phone a lot, and he's always telling me how much he loves me. Many times he's really sweet and sensitive. But when he's with his friends, it's awful! He tells them all about my body parts, and they laugh and ask to talk to me. When this happens, I hang up. Then he calls back and apologizes and begs me to call him back. Sometimes he's in tears when he calls. He *does* have a lot of problems, but I don't want to make excuses for the way he acts. What should I do?

Windsor Locks, Connecticut

DON'T call him back! If he wants to talk with you, (1) he can be a gentleman and speak courteously, and (2) *he* can call *you*.

Sounds like this guy isn't even close to being ready for a relationship with a girl. While he may be sincere in his apology, he's not mature enough to change. Sounds like he needs a counselor, and that's not *your* role in a relationship.

Don't call him. And if he calls you, gently yet firmly tell him it's time to quit seeing each other. You can do much better than a guy who talks about your anatomy to phone-happy friends.

Dear Susie:

My best friend is a boy. We met at a Christian camp and have been friends for about a year. He's a Christian, and we have great discussions on a variety of topics.

I know him really well and think I'm falling in love with him. So what's the problem? He has a girlfriend. I'm afraid if I share my feelings it could jeopardize our wonderful friendship. I've prayed about it a lot, but I still don't know what to do.

Mulino, Oregon

I think you've answered your own question. Since he already has a girlfriend, you may not only jeopardize your friendship with him but also his relationship with his girlfriend. If you're friends with his girlfriend, you could also mess up *that* friendship.

Be grateful for having such a special guy friend. Count his friendship as a terrific gift from God, and realize that the man you eventually marry will probably be your best friend.

You mentioned you've already prayed about this. Great! Now leave it in God's hands, knowing that if he wants your friendship to turn romantic, he'll allow that to happen without hurting three people in the process. His timing is so incredibly perfect.

The relationship with the girl he's dating probably won't last forever, so I encourage you to continue your best-friendship.

HEY! YOU DESERVE
A BREAK
For reading this much. So . . .

- Look up something in the encyclopedia that you've always wanted to know about.
- Get a great devotional book just for girls. It's called *Ready for Prime Time: Devotions for Girls* by Andrea Stephens.
- Get a subscription to *Brio* magazine for teen girls . . . a great way to hear from Susie every single month! You can call 1-800-A-FAMILY and ask for a free sample.
- Memorize Psalm 1. (Don't panic—it's only six verses long.)
- Read a great book called *What Hollywood Won't Tell You about Love, Sex, and Dating* by Greg Johnson and Susie Shellenberger.
- Pretend you're eight years old again and read *The Velveteen Rabbit* by Margery Williams. You can find it in your local library, and you won't have to buy it!

3

GOD AND STUFF

Dear Susie:

My friend believes in reincarnation. She's also a Christian. Is this okay? I'm confused.

Maple Valley, Washington

What *is* a Christian? Someone who has repented of her sins, asked Jesus to reign over her life, committed herself to following Christ with *all* her heart, and someone who believes and follows God's Word.

If your friend *calls* herself a Christian yet doesn't fully believe the Bible, she's only kidding herself. God's Word is crystal clear on reincarnation.

If she's unaware of what God has to say about all this, share Hebrews 9:27 with her: "And just as it is destined that men die only once, and after that comes judgment." How many times do we die? Once.

Ecclesiastes 3:1–2 puts it this way: "There is a right time for everything: A time to be born, a time to die." Notice it doesn't say, "A time to keep dying and living and dying and living."

It doesn't get much clearer than that, does it? There is no such thing as reincarnation.

Dear Susie:

I want to minister to my friend and bring her to the Lord, but she believes in Buddha. How do I do this without offending her?

Kingston, Ontario, Canada

Are you familiar with contemporary Christian artist Karthi? She grew up in India and was raised in the Hindu religion. Though Hinduism and Buddhism are completely different (Hindus believe in many gods; Buddhists believe in one), they're both pretty far from Christianity.

Karthi had a Christian friend who prayed for her consistently. She never tried to force her beliefs on her, but instead she gently explained what she believed and why, whenever it was *appropriate*. In other words, she was careful not to step on Karthi's toes and didn't offend her.

Karthi couldn't help but see the difference in her friend's life. She had a real joy—something that went much deeper than fleeting happiness. And she sensed a real purpose in her friend's life that she knew was missing in her own.

Karthi was so attracted to her *life*, that she began to question her more and more about her beliefs. Eventually they prayed together and Karthi accepted Jesus as her Savior.

Bottom line: Your life will say much more than your words. But have your words ready! Know what you believe and *why*. Work on creating a testimony: what you were like before you met Christ, how you accepted him as your Lord, and the difference he's made in your life after becoming a Christian.

Dear Susie:

My pastor recently resigned, and for no apparent reason. His daughter has been my absolute best friend since the time we were infants. Since I heard this news a few months ago, many of my other friends (and other church members) are saying they're leaving also (due to the resignation).

I feel as though my church—and my life—is falling apart. I've been praying about all this but still want your advice.

Tuscarora, Nevada

I'm sorry you're going through such a tough time. It's always hard when a pastor or staff member resigns. We look to them for spiritual leadership, and we feel a void when they leave.

We serve a God, though, who NEVER leaves us hanging! He has promised to *always* provide for us. It may be hard to believe, but God already has his hand on someone else to fill that important role for your church and in your life.

Sometimes people in the church disagree so sharply on something that it causes a split. This is always damaging. God wants his people to be a *unit,* pulling together—not a divided team. I don't know the details of what happened in your church, but it sounds like there are some hurt feelings.

Remember why you started going to this church. Your family probably felt that's where God led them to worship. Though a pastor contributes greatly to that, he can't be the sole reason you attend. I encourage you to stay where you are and support the new pastor.

Dear Susie:

What do you think is the proper dress for Sunday morning church? Also, what about Sunday night and Wednesday?

Bowie, Maryland

I choose to wear a dress on Sunday morning and evening. Sunday morning just seems a little more formal, and I want to give God my best. This *doesn't* mean those who wear dresses are better Christians than those who don't. God is much more concerned with our *inside* than he is with our *outside*.

Wednesdays are a little different. Sometimes I'm working with the teens and we meet in the church gym. We play games, sing some wild songs, and study the Word. Even though it's a worship experience, it's more informal. Because of all we do, I choose to wear jeans.

WELL, YOU SAID TO WEAR A DRESS TO CHURCH. WHAT'S WRONG NOW?

It really depends on your particular church. Some churches are more formal than others. It also depends on what your parents are comfortable with you wearing. I don't think there's a right or wrong answer. The most important thing is simply being in church.

Dear Susie:

I like David Copperfield (the magician), but most of his tricks seem to be impossible. So, I'm wondering if he's involved in any witchcraft that enables him to do these things.

Council Bluffs, Iowa

David Copperfield is actually an illusionist. And the purpose of an illusion is to make you *think* you're seeing the impossible. That's what makes the whole thing so fascinating. I have not heard that he's involved in witchcraft.

Dear Susie:

Why do some people think youth group is "uncool"? Only three out of the twelve kids in our church come.

Carol Stream, Illinois

Maybe it's not a matter of "uncool"—maybe they're just bored. What happens in a regular youth meeting? Is someone giving a lecture? They probably feel they get enough of that at school. Or is someone leading a lively discussion? Are there fun crowd breakers and thought-provoking challenges?

If your group needs some spice, consider ordering one of the following: *Great Ideas for Small Youth Groups* by Wayne Rice; *Get 'Em Talking* by Mike Yaconelli and Scott Koenigsaecker; *Youth Program Hour Idea Book* by Larry Leonard and Jack McCormick; *Creative Bible Studies for Young Adults* by Denny Rydberg; *The Youth Group Meeting Guide* by Richard W. Bimler.

Dear Susie:

I have given my life to Christ, but I'm not sure he took me. I didn't have the tingly feelings everyone talks about. Did God accept me or not?

Holland, Michigan

You bet he did! Here's your proof: "For he forgave all your sins, and blotted out the charges proved against

you" (Col. 2:13–14).

"I have written this to you who believe in the Son of God so that you may know you have eternal life" (1 John 5:13).

Pretty exciting, huh? In fact, the Bible tells us that when someone becomes a Christian all of heaven rejoices! In other words, there was some big-time partying going on just because of *you!* Your name is now written in the Book of Life.

You say you didn't feel anything when you asked Jesus to come into your heart. Know what? That's okay. Some people feel something; others don't. I didn't. Don't base your relationship with Christ on *feeling,* ground it in *faith.*

You don't always feel the sun, but you know it's there. You don't always feel the wind, but you know the air still exists. And on cloudy days, when you can't even see the sun, you know it's still there. It works the same way with God. You won't always feel him, but *faith* tells you he's here. Why? Because he *promised* he'd never leave you! (Check out Deut. 31:6; Josh. 1:5; and Heb. 13:5.)

There's a little booklet called *Your Most Important Relationship* that explains this in more detail. You can get one for only fifteen cents by writing or calling Youth for Christ, P.O. Box 228822, Denver, CO 80222; 303-843-9000.

Dear Susie:

I have a friend who hasn't accepted God yet. I'm trying to think of a way to let her know that God loves her without scaring her away or making her mad at me. What should I do?

Moorhead, Missouri

Wow! It's neat that you care about where your friend spends eternity. And I admire the fact that you don't want to be pushy or offensive to her. I wrote a book with Greg Johnson called *Keeping Your Cool While Sharing Your Faith.* You might want to check it out because it's full of great ways to help your non-Christian friends.

The most important thing, though, is to make sure *you're* living a Christlike example in front of her. She needs to see Jesus in your life. Invite her to youth activities and church services, and pray daily for God to give you a convenient opportunity to talk with her about your beliefs. Know what? *He will.* And when the situation arises, gently share the difference God is making in your life.

Dear Susie:

Do you think Christians can be models or be in beauty pageants? I think that would be a lot of fun, but some people in my church don't think it's right.

Detroit, Michigan

I believe God can use our testimony wherever we are. Stephanie Irving, Miss Colorado 1993–94 is a member of my church, and she uses her platform to take a stand for strong values. I believe God is using her to boldly impact others.

Contemporary Christian artist Kim Boyce was the 1983 Miss Florida and a top-10 Miss America finalist in 1984. God used her then—and still is—in her music.

Laura Krauss and her husband Jeff Calenberg are top New York models. They're in demand all over the nation. Yet they use their influence for God. They initiated a Models for Christ group, have an active ministry to the homeless of New York City, and have been known to ask those in charge of photo shoots with food involved if they can deliver the leftovers to the hungry.

I think it all comes down to our hearts. We have to question our motives—that's what God is concerned about. He's also concerned about compromise. Anything we're involved in becomes wrong when we compromise our relationship with Christ.

Dear Susie:

Everyone at church is always telling the teens that we should read our Bibles on a daily basis. But where do I start? Do I need a devotional book? If so, is there one you recommend? Should I really read my Bible *every* day? Also, what *is* a walk with God? Please explain this stuff to me.

Bayshore, New York

It's important that reading your Bible become a good habit. The adults are telling you this because they want to see it become a solid discipline with you. For instance, you brush your teeth every day. (I hope!) It's a routine. It's a good habit you've developed because you know it's good for you.

It works the same with the Bible. To be spiritually healthy, we need to read God's Word consistently. The Gospel of John is a good place to begin. Do you have a Bible you understand? There are several student versions available at your local Christian bookstore. They're filled with cool designs and neat situation stories to introduce you to certain passages. They also help you learn how to relate the Scripture to your everyday life.

If you're interested in a devotional book, there are several written just for teens. Keep in mind, though, that a devotional book shouldn't take the place of reading the Bible. God's Word is your ultimate devo book. Check out the suggested reading list at the back of the book for some student Bibles and devotional books you might be interested in.

What is a walk with God? It's a relationship. Just as you make time for your school and church friends, make time for Jesus—your *best* friend. Talk with him, read his letter to you, and listen for his voice.

Dear Susie:

I have been a Christian for a long time, and I still haven't gotten to know God as my personal friend and Father. Any advice?

New Castle, Delaware

Imagine Jamie is one of your best friends. She says she wants to go shopping with you on Saturday. But she gets busy and you have to go alone. When you see her at school she says she'll call you tonight, but she doesn't. When you run into her at the pep assembly the next day, she says, "I really want to get together this week; I've just been really busy. But how about grabbing a pizza after Friday's game?"

You eagerly look forward to Friday and enjoy the game. But afterward, Jamie runs off with some other friends. You might begin to doubt just how close you really are.

Well, it works much the same way with Christ. Imagine how he must feel when we rush off to school every day without first spending some time with him. Then we quickly breathe a prayer and beg for his help before the science test, but later that night we get involved in a couple of TV shows and don't make time for him before going to bed.

45

God desires a close relationship with you. In fact, he wants to be your best friend, your Savior, your guide, your energizer, your *everything*. He wants to be NUMBER ONE. That's what a 100 percent commitment is all about.

So determine to read your Bible some every day; talk with him and watch for his leading in your life. The more time you spend together, the closer you'll become.

Dear Susie:

The Bible says we should be humble, but I heard it's good to have high self-esteem. How can I be humble and still think highly of myself?

Boston, Massachusetts

You're right. This is kind of confusing. Joshua 1:7 tells us to be strong, confident, and brave. Ephesians 4:2 encourages us to be gentle and humble. I like the way Romans 12:16 says it: "Work happily together. Don't try to act big. Don't try to get into the good graces of important people, but enjoy the company of ordinary folks. And don't think you know it all!"

In other words, we shouldn't think too highly of ourselves. Yes, God wants us to feel good about ourselves and to have a healthy self-image, but he doesn't want us to get carried away thinking we're better than someone else.

Dear Susie:

I want people to see my Christianity. How do I deal with frustration and still keep a smile on my face?

Milwaukee, Oregon

Maybe you *don't* need to keep a smile on your face when you're frustrated. God doesn't want you to be a phony. Jesus wasn't. He showed what he felt. Your non-Christian friends need to see how you handle problems.

Instead of acting happy when you're not, be genuine. I'm not telling you to scream and yell and throw a temper tantrum, but when something frustrates you, it's okay to acknowledge that.

For instance, let's say you're having a problem with the grade you received on your history test. Which would be the best (and honest) way for a Christian to handle the matter:

"Wow. I failed another history test. I studied for three hours, but hey, it's not gonna get *me* down! Anyone wanna get some ice cream?"

"You know, I just don't understand why Mr. Baker counted my answer wrong, and it kinda ticks me off. Think I'll go talk to him about it."

"Stupid jerk! That lousy Baker should've never been hired. Where'd he get his teaching credentials anyway, out of a Cracker Jack box?"

The second response, obviously, is honest and real. Be careful not to blow up in front of those you're trying to witness to, but allow them to see you're human—you face the same problems they do. The difference? Christ helps you handle them better.

Dear Susie:

Can a young Christian lady preach but not be a preacher?

Marysville, Washington

47

I speak about every other weekend all over the nation for youth groups, youth retreats, and youth revivals. I've never been to seminary and don't consider myself a preacher, but I love to communicate God's Word to teens.

Some denominations will not ordain women to be preachers. Some will. The church I belong to *does* ordain women to be preachers. I have chosen not to be ordained because I consider myself more of a speaker simply sharing God's Word than a preacher.

Dear Susie:

Judging from a simple walk down the street, Satan really has his works planted in this world. Magazines like *Playboy* and *Penthouse* litter newsstands, vulgar words float everywhere, and movies are steadily getting worse. This stuff is easy to watch out for, but New Age is a confusing one to figure out.

What *is* New Age and its products?

Ramsey, North Dakota

New Age can be very confusing to Christians because they believe *some* of the same things we do. They believe in God and think it's important to develop yourself spiritually. They also emphasize discipline and encourage each other to become the best they can be.

There are many facets of various New Age beliefs, but some things *all* New Agers have in common are:

- They all believe in some form of reincarnation.
- They all believe that we are in the process of becoming gods.
- They all believe that God is evidenced everywhere. In other words, he's inside this paper, on that tree, in my pencil, within your desk.

This belief is also stretched to include that "God-power" being available to us through channelers, crystals, and mediums.

As Christians, we believe that God is contacted through prayer—a personal conversation with Jesus Christ. We don't need a piece of rock or another object to get through to him. Nor are we power-hungry disciples seeking to be equal with him.

The Bible tells us in 1 John 4:1–3 to beware of false teachers and teachings that sound good. New Age is a false teaching. And where does falsehood originate? From Satan.

Keep your eyes glued on Jesus, and your heart grounded in his Word.

Dear Susie:

How can I get into missionary work?

Alexandria, Louisiana

First, check with your pastor to see what your own church denomination has to offer. If you think God is calling you to full-time missionary service as a career, but you're not sure, consider getting involved in a summer missions project just for teens. Here are a few organizations that offer teen programs:

Teen Missions, 885 East Hall Road, Dept. TMT, Merritt Island, FL 32953-8443, 407-453-0350

Youth with a Mission, P.O. Box 55309, Seattle, WA 98155, 206-363-9844

World Servants, 8233 Gator Lane #6, West Palm Beach, FL 33411, 407-790-0800

Missions Outreach, Inc., P.O. Box 73, Bethany, MO 64424, 816-425-2277

Teen World Outreach, 7245 College Street, Lima, NY 14485, 716-582-2790

Project Serve, Youth for Christ U.S.A., P.O. Box 228822, Denver, CO 80222, 303-843-9000

Janz Team, 2121 Henderson Highway, Winnipeg, Manitoba, Canada, R2G 1P8, 204-334-0055

Teen Mania Ministries, P.O. Box 700721, Tulsa, OK 74170-0721, 1-800-299-TEEN

GUY BREAK!

Dear Susie:

I go to a Christian school, and there's this really cute guy in my class that I like (as friends). But whenever I say hi to him in the hallway everyone accuses me of *liking* him. Know what I mean? I really want to call him and talk with him (as *friends*), but I'm sure he'd think I'm a dork. What should I do?

Goodrich, Michigan

This is gonna be hard for you to accept, but *don't* call him. Is it hard to accept the fact that if he wants to talk with you, he'll call? Maybe you're thinking, *Yeah, but if I don't call him, he won't call me because he's not going to make the first move.* Hmmmm. Then what does that tell you?

Any guy who is *really* interested in establishing a friendship (on any level) with a girl will eventually do something about it. It may take him longer than you'd like, but *if* he wants to get to know you better, he will eventually do something about it.

If not? Accept the fact he's not interested in a friendship with you right now, and set your sights on someone else who is.

Dear Susie:

My family has been living in the same town for three years. For two and a half of those years I've liked this guy. Our parents are good friends, and that means we get together a lot.

Two years ago it was a crush. A year ago we started becoming friends. This year I've felt differently about him. When he's gone, I miss him. I think about him a lot, and

51

when we're together I get this funny fluttery feeling in my stomach. Is this love?

Lincoln, Nebraska

Well . . . it's obvious that you like him much more than just a friend. You have special feelings for him—romantic feelings. But many people confuse love with feelings. Though feelings are a *part* of love—there's also a whole lot more. Love is commitment . . . and it's also a decision.

What you're experiencing is exciting, and since the two of you "click," your friendship will probably blossom into something a little deeper. But let's hold off for now on calling it *love*.

Too many teens make the mistake of telling their boy/girlfriend they "love" them, when they're really just in love with love. It feels good to date, to be treated special, to have someone care about you and pay attention to you. And it's very easy to fall in love with *that*.

WELL, IT'S EITHER LOVE OR THAT SUPER COMBO PIZZA I JUST ATE.

What you're feeling is real, but can you feel comfortable calling it "deep like"? Real love means you're committing yourself to that person. And though you may commit yourselves to a dating relationship, chances are there will be other guys you'll also date during the next five years.

Enjoy your friendship with this special guy . . . but save your "I love you" phrase for the man you want to spend the rest of your life with.

4

THE BLACKBOARD JUNGLE

Dear Susie:

We have a new teacher this year at school, and he's really weird. The other day during class he was staring at me kind of funny, then he came over and started playing with my hair and rubbing my neck. This really frightened me.

A few days later, he did this to my best friend. Now we're afraid to go to his class. I hate him, and he didn't even do much to me.

Abilene, Texas

This teacher did *way* too much to you! He crossed over a line he should have never been near. I'm so sorry this happened to you and your friend. NO ONE should have to be scared to go to class, but it's certainly understandable why you and your friend are.

I wonder how many other students he's touched? Please, please, please don't let him get away with this. Talk to your principal immediately. Teachers are hired to teach—not to frighten students by crossing suggestive physical lines.

Dear Susie:

I'm having trouble with a teacher at school. Everything I do seems to make her mad. What do you think I should do to get along with her better?

Kansas City, Kansas

What's "everything" you do? While she's giving notes, do you ask "Is this going to be on the test?" Are you tardy to class? Do you ask to be excused for water or the rest room often? After she's made an assignment, are you asking questions about things she's already explained? Do you complain about homework, or have you ever accused her of being unfair? If so, then as a former high school teacher, I can understand her frustration.

If you *haven't* done any of these things, she may be having a bad day (or year!) and taking it out on you. And that's not fair.

But one thing's clear: you'll never know what the problem is unless you talk with her. Ask her (after school when she's not rushed for the next class) if there's a convenient time you can stop by to talk. Then when you do chat with her, begin by explaining that you respect her and want to get the most out of her class that you can.

Explain that you feel she's frustrated with you, and ask her if there's something specific you're doing that she would prefer you wouldn't. This puts the responsibility in her lap. If you are at fault, she has an opportunity to share with you what kind of improvement is in order.

If you're not at fault, she has the chance to explain the "wall" or what *is* going on. It could be she's having some personal problems at home. Don't expect her to open up and give you her troubles, but you *do* deserve some kind of affirmation or explanation.

Dear Susie:

My teacher counted some of my assignments as F's. They were turned in on time, and the answers were correct. She just said she couldn't read them—that I wrote too small. All the assignments in my other classes were written in the same writing. Can she do this?

Cranston, Rhode Island

Has she ever announced to the class that if she couldn't read the assignment she wouldn't grade it? If so, then you'll have to play by her rules.

If she's never mentioned anything about your handwriting to you before, and if you've been turning in assignments like this all year long, then ask if you can talk with her after class.

Explain that you worked hard on your papers, and tell her you weren't aware that you could receive an F for your penmanship. Ask her if you can recopy the assignment over using better handwriting.

57

If she absolutely refuses to budge, then make an appointment to talk with your school counselor. Meanwhile . . . try to write bigger—not just for her class, but for your personal success in life. No one enjoys having to squint and decipher something that's too much work to read.

Have you thought of typing your work or using a computer? If you don't own one, maybe your school has one you can use at specific times. Computers are fun and typing is great preparation for college.

Dear Susie:

I'm having a problem with one of my coaches. She yells at me. One day I cried. I'm scared that if I say something to her, I won't be able to play on the team anymore. Please help.

Nashville, Tennessee

Unfortunately, some coaches use this technique for demanding excellence on the court. You (like many others) don't respond well to intimidation and pressure. That's okay. Sports should be an enjoyable, fun experience for you—not a tension-filled activity that is so pressured that you're scared to perform for chance of failing.

It sounds like this is simply her style, just the way she

coaches. I doubt talking with her would do any good. She's probably not going to change her coaching tactics because a player tells her she doesn't like to be yelled at.

I think you're going to have to make a decision: Is this particular sport important enough to you that you can grit your teeth and bear it in order to play?

If sports isn't a major passion of yours, throw your time and energy into something else you enjoy doing.

Dear Susie:

How can I stick up for a teacher I really like, but who is abused verbally by the class?

Norfolk, Virginia

I admire your willingness to go against the flow! Sometimes teachers aren't given a fair shake, and that's just as wrong as a student being misjudged.

It will be hard, but when others are reaming out your teacher during class, stand your ground and express *your* views. If they're being unfair, say so! You may feel you're the only one in the class who holds this opinion, but who knows? When *you* dare to speak out, others (who agree with you) may take courage and back up what you're saying. I know several teachers across the nation who would *love* to have you in class!

Dear Susie:

How can I tell my teacher about my relationship with Christ?

Yazoo, Mississippi

One of the strongest ways you can tell her is by *living* it. Dare to be Jesus to your teacher. Smile a lot. Say hi to her when passing in the hall. If you can enter class early, take the time to ask about her weekend. When she looks nice, compliment her.

As you get to know her better, you'll find opportunities to "sneak in" comments about your church and your beliefs. If your church is having a special service, invite her. She'd probably appreciate knowing you'd like to have her there.

When I was a junior in high school, I was in a business class in which the students *hated* the teacher. (I don't mean dislike—I mean *hate!*) They openly expressed this to her—by saying things like "I hate you!" It was really sad.

There was another girl in the class with me who attended my church. We determined to love her in spite of how the rest of the class acted. You know what? People can't help but respond to love!

Our church youth choir did a big musical drama toward the end of the school year, so we invited her to come. She did! And guess what? Every so often she continued to visit—and even brought her boyfriend!

She responded to our invitation because she knew we were genuine—and could sense that we really cared about her—not just as a teacher, but as a person.

Dear Susie:

There's this girl at school named Beth, but everyone calls her Merle. She follows me around and really bugs me. She recently had a party for the eighth-grade girls and no one came.

I know the Christian thing to do would have been to go, but I didn't. I was afraid she would follow me more. How can I tell her to get lost in a nice way?

Southlake, Texas

Get lost in a nice way? There's *not* a nice way to tell someone to get lost! What would Jesus do? He'd let her follow him around, wouldn't he? Think the lepers were cool to hang out with? Nope. Think it helped his reputation to be seen with the woman at the well? Nope. Think people respected him *more* because he hung out with thieves and tax collectors and the outcasts of society? Nope. He befriended the people nobody else would get near.

I know it's hard. And I'm not saying you need to become Beth's best friend or hang out with her all the time or invite her over to your house. I *am* saying that though she's not as cool as you, *you're* not as cool as someone else. And you don't want anyone running away from you, do you?

Be Jesus to her. If she sits down at your lunch table, don't ignore her, talk to her. Be friendly. Smile at her. Listen to her. You may be the only positive influence in her life.

And check out the following verses before you go to bed tonight, okay? Matthew 5:46–48; Romans 12:2–3, 9–10, 16; 1 Corinthians 13 (yep, the whole chapter!); James 2:1–4, 14–17; 1 John 3:18.

GUY BREAK!

Dear Susie:

How can I tell my friend that she does "too much" with guys? She always just laughs off whatever I say.

Sounds like she's not too willing to listen to anyone right now. But there are several excellent Christian teen books and videos on the market that deal with this very subject. Consider ordering a copy of *Life, Sex and Everything in Between,* by Bill Sanders from your local Christian bookstore. Try one of two things: you read it first, then ask her to read it; or try reading and discussing it together.

Your friend may not be aware of the danger there is in being sexually loose. She may not know that even though condoms are promoted for "safe sex," they're really not safe at all. For instance, the HIV virus is 450 times *smaller* than a sperm. Condoms and the spread of AIDS have been compared to water going through a fishnet. Why would *anyone* want to trust her life to a flimsy piece of latex?

Hopefully, when she realizes that there is no such thing as safe sex outside of marriage, she'll think twice about her sexual escapades.

Dear Susie:

I'm thirteen years old and have been praying about this sixteen-year-old guy at church. I know he's the one I'm supposed to marry, but nothing's happening. Did I misunderstand God? Am I just going to have to wait? What's going on?

Mountain Home A.F.B., Idaho

62

How do you know he's the one you're supposed to marry? I admire the fact that you're praying about it . . . but could it be you want him so bad, you're assuming it's God's will?

If he really is who you are to marry, wouldn't God also reveal this to *him?* Many women have chased men off (whom they could have had a meaningful relationship with) because they put too much pressure on them by sharing false messages supposedly from God.

I'm guessing that you really want to have a boyfriend— or at least that's what your letter sounds like. What if God doesn't want you dating *anyone* right now? Can you accept that?

I don't want to say, "Yes, you've misinterpreted God," but the bottom line is that God wants you to focus on Jesus more than on this guy.

OKAY ... ENOUGH'S
ENOUGH!
STOP FOR A WHILE.
TAKE A BREATHER.
In other words,
put this book down
before the words start to ooze out your ears.

- Smile at your elbow.
- Be kind to a napkin.
- Find out who invented the graham cracker.
- Ask Mom if we can have pizza tonight. (Tell her *I* want thin crust pepperoni with extra pepperoni.)
- Stare at your ceiling, sing your fave top-40 tune, chew a wad of orange gum, and do fifty jumping jacks all at the same time. *(Betcha can't do it!)*
- File your nails . . . and yes, throw the trimmings *away*.
- Develop a new smile.
- Write a note to your youth leader *right now* telling how much you appreciate him or her.
- You didn't write the note, did you? Do it *now*.
- Okay, if you're not gonna write the note, you might as well keep reading.

5

HOW CAN I FEEL BETTER ABOUT MYSELF?

Dear Susie:
I feel like a nerd a lot. I'm not sure anyone likes me, and I wear glasses that break easily. I want to try some new things on how to make more friends. Can you give me some tips?

San Juan Capistrano, California

Thanks for the picture you sent me! You're a beautiful young lady. I put your photo on my bulletin board, and when one of my staff saw it, *he* grabbed it and pinned it on *his* bulletin board! So, besides fighting over your photo, we both think you're absolutely *terrif!*

I think your glasses look classy . . . but if you're wanting a change, perhaps you can talk with your mom about the cost of contacts.

Tips on friendship? My suggestions: Smile a lot (like in your picture), be consistently kind, and don't be afraid to invite others to your house for fun times.

There are several Christian teen books on the market about friendships, but I'm sending you one called *Dear Diary . . . The Secret Feelings of a Junior High Girl* by Pat Baker.

Dear Susie:

I am convinced that I have a problem. I don't think I'm human. *This isn't a prank!* See, I never get excited or nervous. I rarely smile and never get emotional.

My friends consider me mature. I *am* mature, but I go beyond maturity. I'm intelligent and rational; yet when it comes to feelings, I have none. What's wrong with me?

St. Paul, Minnesota

I think it's great that you're wanting to get in touch with your feelings—and they *are* there, it's just that they're out of reach right now. That must be terribly frustrating.

It's my guess that one of two things is happening.

1. You've been through a traumatic experience that has caused you to build a wall of protection around your emotions. Expressing them would seem like a dam bursting—it would be overwhelming. Not showing any feeling could be your way of helping you handle the tough stuff in your life.

2. You've never paid attention to feelings because you're a very rational left-brain person. As you may know, our brain is divided into two halves. The left brain excels in details, organization, numbers, and logic. You're probably good at math and science. The right brain excels in creativity, imagination, and the arts.

Also, maybe there's not much emotion expressed in your family. That doesn't mean it's not there; it simply means you may need to *work* at developing this other side of your personality.

I suggest you let someone help you uncover your feelings. Can you talk with a counselor, youth pastor, or minister?

Though you say you have no feelings, you also *feel* like an alien. Share this with your parents. Perhaps together, you can learn to develop this exciting part of your personality!

Dear Susie:

I'm very shy around my youth group. I just can't get out of my shell to talk and joke around like the others do. I'd like to go to the activities and outings, but I'd just be in a corner by myself. How can I make friends?

Delta, British Columbia, Canada

Are you familiar with contemporary Christian artist Margaret Becker? She told me that she used to be very shy in junior high. One day, though, she just *determined*—no matter how hard it was—to act friendly. And at first, it *was* kind of an act, because she was too frightened to actually feel it.

"I made myself come to school early," she says. "I stood by the door and started saying hi to people as they walked into the building. I sort of became the 'school greeter,'" she laughs.

Guess what happened? As she continued to reach out, kept saying hi, and asking questions to get a conversation started, her feelings eventually caught up with her actions; she actually began to enjoy meeting new people. It didn't happen quickly, but she finally broke out of her shy shell.

You may need to do something just as drastic. Force yourself to say hi to someone in your youth group. I know you'll feel like you're going to pass out, but you really won't. I promise.

Will you also consider talking with your youth leader one-on-one? Explain the problem and ask him or her to pray with you about your shyness.

God didn't create everyone to be the life of the party, but check out what he says in 2 Timothy 1:7: "For the Holy Spirit, God's gift, does not want you to be afraid of people, but to be wise and strong, and to love them and enjoy being with them."

Dear Susie:
I have been struggling with a very difficult problem for about a year now: conceit. Many people (guys *and* girls) have told me how pretty I am. I've gotten used to guys asking me out all the time and staring when I walk past. Now I can't help but admire myself in the mirror or in photographs. I feel terrible. What can I do?

Atlanta, Georgia

It sounds like you're basing your idea of who you are on what other people tell you. This means you don't have an accurate picture of yourself from the eyes of God.

It's real important that you learn to separate the two (how others see you vs. how God sees you), so you can develop your personal view of yourself on what God sees (because that's the *real* picture). Society says that you have to wear certain clothes or weigh a certain amount to be pretty, but God's *truth* says you're worth *so much* in his eyes that he even knows the exact number of hairs on your head. As you work on meshing your view of you with God's view of you, you won't be puffed up by what others say.

Keep in mind that your good looks can change in a matter of seconds! A car wreck, boating accident, or any number of injuries can forever alter your looks. But character and inner beauty are lasting qualities.

Also keep in mind that *no one* likes a person who's caught up in herself: always looking in the mirror, primping, etc. Sounds like you're pretty close to being there. Wouldn't you rather guys ask you out because they enjoy being with *you*, instead of simply being turned on by looks that could quickly change?

That's pretty surface.

Dear Susie:
I have a problem responding to guys. They come up to me and start talking, but I don't cooperate. The minute it comes

69

to asking me out, I make an excuse or say something like, "I have to go."

Maybe I'm afraid of something; I don't know. I get along okay with my male cousin and his friend, so I don't think I'm afraid of boys—I even go to the beach or cycling with them.

Maybe I have trouble believing a guy would really like me. I'm not sure *what* the problem is. But at the rate I'm going now, I'm afraid I may never get serious with a guy.

Madison, Wisconsin

It's okay not to be serious with a guy! In fact, it's really smarter to wait a few years for that. You're probably more comfortable with your cousin and his friend because you *know* them and you're around them more.

It's hard to be around *anyone* we don't know well. There's an element of insecurity in all of us . . . so you're not alone!

I think it's great that guys approach you. That proves they want to be with you and get to know you better. Shouldn't that tell you that you're "good enough"? Not only are you good enough, you're great! Know why? Because you were made in God's image. Hmmmm. That makes you pretty special!

It seems you're the most nervous when you suspect a guy is getting ready to ask you out. Let's chat for a sec about "going out," okay? Are you building too much into that phrase? Maybe you're thinking *serious date.* Try, instead, to think in terms of just doing something fun with a friend—like cycling, bowling, a few rounds of mini-golf, grabbing a burger, watching a video.

If you think of things like these, it'll take some of the pressure off. Also, remember that when a guy asks you out, you can have as much control of the evening as you want.

For instance, he says, "Are you busy Friday night?" You can say, "No," and let him suggest what he had in mind, or you can respond with a preplanned idea. "Well, I was kind of wanting to see this new video that's out. Wanna join me for popcorn and Coke at my house?"

This puts the evening in your own environment, where you're more secure and feel more comfortable. It also assures you of other people being there—your family or other friends if you want to invite them.

I also want to mention that it's possible you only *think* guys are getting ready to ask you out, when they might just be trying to get to know you better. Nothing wrong with having more friends. Don't assume the worst. Relax, smile, and make as many friends as you can.

GUY BREAK!

Dear Susie:

There's this guy who really likes me, and deep down inside I like him too. But I tell him I *don't* like him . . . because I'm popular and he's not. I don't want to ruin my reputation. What do I do?

Candia, New Hampshire

How would *you* feel if a guy *you* liked wouldn't return your interest because you weren't "good enough for him"? That's exactly what you're doing—by denying your feelings based on how popular he is, you're implying that you're better than he is.

Sounds like you're not ready for a relationship yet. Talk with someone who can help you understand what true friendship and *real* values are all about.

Dear Susie:

I really like this great Christian guy, and he's on my mind twenty-four hours a day. I feel empty if I don't have the chance to talk to him on the phone or see him.

He *has* a girlfriend, but that doesn't matter to me—I just want us to be really good friends.

Before I met him, there were times when I was bored, but I could always find things to do. But *now* when I'm bored, I sit around waiting. For what? I don't know! Everything makes me think of him. Sometimes I get so depressed I start to cry. Help!

Willowdale, Ontario, Canada

Wow. Sounds like you *do* want more than to simply be this guy's friend. People don't think about their *friends* twenty-four hours a day, nor do they cry if they can't talk to their friends on the phone. If he means this

72

much to you, he's more than a wanna-be friend . . . he's becoming an obsession.

Since you mentioned that he's a Christian, can I assume you attend the same church, and that *you*, too, are a Christian? You probably already know this, but (sometimes we *all* need to be reminded) God wants to be number one in your life. He wants you to be consumed with *him*. Anyone who takes up more of our time and thoughts than God is someone who is becoming more important than God in our lives.

My advice is to talk with your pastor or youth leader about strengthening your relationship with Christ. Just think, if you could transfer all that energy and attention to Jesus . . . wow! There'd be no stopping how he could impact those around you!

6

THIS ISN'T RIGHT!

Dear Susie:

My boyfriend, Ryan, is very mad at me. We've been to several parties together, and at each one he's slapped me. I forgave him and we went on with life.

But now he's threatening me. He said that he was going to hurt me very badly, and that he'd make sure I was sorry I ever got involved with him. He's really scaring me, and he's strong enough to carry out his threat.

All of my school friends hate him, but I can't find it in my heart to do the same. I still care for him deeply, and during class when we look at each other, I can tell he still cares for me. I don't know what to do anymore.

Eureka, California

This is pretty basic: BREAK UP!

You deserve *much* better! (If you have trouble believing that, please seek professional counseling.)

Don't keep this problem a secret. Talk with your parents or school counselor. You may need help in protecting yourself. A guy with a big temper problem is no one to take lightly.

Dear Susie:

About a year ago I was raped by an ex-boyfriend. I still have a hard time dealing with it and have regular nightmares about what happened. I just keep replaying it over and over in my mind.

I feel dirty and used. Everyone in our school knows, and they make fun of me. They say I'm lying and I deserved it! I'm a strong Christian and don't understand why this is happening.

Detroit, Michigan

How very alone you must feel. I am so sorry. I wish I could erase the past year for you. Can you find comfort in knowing that God's heart breaks *with* yours? Psalm 34 tells us he is very close to those whose hearts are breaking. Take refuge in this.

You have expressed some strong feelings of isolation. You're getting no strength or understanding from kids at school, and this will simply eat away at you if you don't talk with someone who will listen—really listen— and help you escape the nightmares and isolation. Letting it out is one of the first steps of healing.

Though some may say you deserved this, the bottom line is *no one, absolutely no one,* deserves to be taken advantage of. You're not to blame. It's not your fault. You're dealing with a lot of shame, and that's another reason why it's important to find someone (an adult whom you trust) to talk with. I suggest your parents, a local counselor, or your pastor.

There may be support groups in your area that could help. You may also want to consider going to a rape crisis counseling center (look in the yellow pages), switching schools, and talking to your folks about pressing charges.

Though it may seem impossible, God has the power and the desire to make something good happen from this nightmare. Keep turning it over to the One who really understands.

Dear Susie:

About two years ago my mom remarried. This guy is a real JERK. He and my mom fight about me all the time. He tells her I'm a bum and white trash and that he doesn't ever want to become family with me! He's not physically abusive, but I feel I'm being verbally abused.

I know you're going to say, "Talk with your mom about it." Believe me, I have—many times! It doesn't help. What should I do?

Gillette, Wyoming

I wish I could take you out for a blue Icee and tell you everything will be better tomorrow, but it probably won't. I'm sorry you're living in such a battlefield at home.

Sounds like your stepdad isn't comfortable with all he inherited when he married your mom. But like it or not, he—and you—are part of each other's family now.

Since talking with your mom hasn't helped, I wonder what would happen if you really shocked your stepdad by asking to treat him to dinner?

Save some money, and take him out to one of his favorite spots to eat. There's something unique that happens around food—our guard comes down. It's hard to be really angry at someone over a table in a restaurant, especially when you know they've sacrificed to buy your dinner.

Use this opportunity to tell him you really *want* to improve your relationship. Ask him what, specifically, *you* can do to make things better. Listen and don't be defensive. When he's finished, ask if you, your mom, *and* he can start praying together each evening.

WOW! Wonder what kind of difference that could make! Try it and let me know, okay?

If you continue to have problems, maybe you could suggest that your family go to a counselor together to talk things out.

Dear Susie:

Please help me! I've been molested by my older brother for seven years. I'm fourteen now, and I'm so confused. Whose fault is it? Am I somehow egging him on? What can I do?

I can't talk to anyone because they'll tell my parents and ruin my brother's life. He's so smart and talented. The confusing thing is he's my idol. I've always respected and looked up to him.

I'm afraid he won't respect me if I do something about this. I'm so scared. He hurts me. I freeze. It's like the person inside my body is in this clear box that can see and hear what's going on, but I can't make my body make him stop.

Does God hate me? Am I the one to blame? Is he? Are we both?

I can't even relate to anyone anymore. I can't hold a boyfriend, and I just can't be myself.

What can I do? We just moved to a new city—two thousand miles away from our old home, and I can't trust anyone.

Will I go to hell if I kill myself?

Grant, Wisconsin

First of all, no, it's not your fault! Your brother has stolen from you. He has invaded your innermost privacy. This is *his* fault, and it's important that you place the blame where it belongs.

You've done some good things to protect yourself. For instance, when you say your body is frozen, you've actually built a defense that has equipped you to cope with what's happening on the outside.

I understand not wanting to tell anyone for fear that everyone will turn on you, but there are those who will *not* turn. There has to be someone you can tell. You're right—there are people you *can't* tell; this isn't something you share in the halls between classes. But watch for someone you can trust. Let's begin praying that God will bring an adult into your life that you'll feel comfortable sharing this secret with. You *have* to tell.

I know you feel there is no hope; that you're absolutely at the very end of your rope. You don't know which way to turn. But there *are* places to turn. There *is* hope. There *are* places to go for help—good, solid, healing help.

You say your brother won't respect you if you do anything about this. But he is not treating you with the respect you deserve *now*. You *must* tend to your own needs before you pay attention to the needs of others.

And that's another reason you need to talk with someone—you need help walking through this. You need someone (preferably your parents) who can help you feel safe again.

So please . . . keep looking. Meanwhile, know that I am holding you up to our Father in prayer.

Dear Susie:

I really like this guy, but he won't have anything to do with me because his parents don't think he should be in a relationship with a girl. What should I do? I really like him!

Winston-Salem, North Carolina

Let him go! First of all, why would you want to encourage *anyone* to go against their parents' wishes? That only spells trouble. You want the parents of the guys you date to like you and respect you, right? So, prove that you can be trusted by trying not to stay out too late with your friends, by dressing modestly, and by showing an interest in his (the guy's) family.

Second, he *could* be using his parents as an excuse because it may be too difficult for him to tell you he's just not interested. Either way, back off.

Dear Susie:

I don't have a steady boyfriend right now, but I'm looking for one. How do I know if a guy is right for me?

Watertown, South Dakota

I always encourage girls *and* guys to date someone with similar standards. For me, the most important thing is his relationship with Christ. Is he a Christian? If not, I'm not interested in forming a dating relationship with him. I may play tennis or grab a Coke with him, but I'm very choosy about whom I develop a dating relationship with.

Do you have similar beliefs? I realize no one will agree with everything you believe, but shouldn't there be a few basics that are nailed down? For instance, you don't drink? Good. Don't date guys who do. Grades are important to you? Don't form a relationship with someone who

80

ditches school and cheats. You're taking a stand against R-rated movies? Terrific. Date guys who won't ask you to attend.

I'M LOOKING FOR A STEADY BOYFRIEND.

When you compromise your own standards for someone else, it's too easy to fall into temptation. Keep your values high, and look for those who have similar standards.

Dear Susie:

My only friend is a twelve-year-old boy. We can almost read each other's thoughts and feelings. Is this wrong?

Florence, Oregon

Well, if you're twenty-one years old I'm going to worry. Since you didn't say how old you are, I'll assume you're pretty close in age, okay?

Sounds like you have a great friendship. Nothing wrong with that. What *does* concern me, though, is the fact that you only have one friend. If you're excluding others just so you can constantly hang out with him, then I encourage you to be more well-rounded in your friendships. *Any* friendship that becomes exclusive is questionable.

I'll bet you're a blast to be around. Will you think about reaching out to other girls your age? Invite them over for a night of videos and popcorn. By only having one friend, other people are missing out on a great friendship with *you!*

YEP, HERE IT IS.
Break time!

- Take your shoes off, and put them back on again.
- Go back to the first question in the book, and without rereading the answer, write your own.
- Call a friend.
- Go look in your closet for stuff you don't wear anymore, and ask your parents if you can donate to charity.
- Pray for your pastor.
- Wash your hands backward.
- Make up a word, then ask a friend to create a definition.
- Eat a piece of raw spaghetti.
- Surprise your mom by vacuuming the house without being asked!

7

IT'S GETTING HARD TO RAISE MY PARENTS!

Dear Susie:
I'm a fourteen-year-old high school sophomore living with my dad and stepmom. Dad hates me. He only talks to me when I do something wrong. This makes me want to hate him back. I'm so stressed, I started smoking again.

He yells at me for not eating, for hanging out with college kids, and for being with my boyfriend. I eat when I'm hungry, the people I hang out with are my friends, and I love my boyfriend.

I'm so cold inside. I write depressing poetry and am dangerously close to running away with my boyfriend and his friends to New York.

I pray my dad gets close to the Lord and finds happiness. He still hates me, though. What's wrong with me?

Mohrsville, Pennsylvania

You *say* you're cold inside . . . but you're *packed* with intense emotions! You're feeling confused, desperate, and angry. Before we start at the top of your list, let me say that running away is *never* the answer! The media is filled with real-life stories of teens living on the street who experience danger, extreme poverty, and many times death!

Are you sure your dad *hates* you? That's such a strong word! Could it be that you're interpreting his parental warnings as a desire to make your life miserable?

Try writing a letter to your dad . . . not to give to him right away, but as a means of looking at your feelings and getting them on paper. Perhaps at a later time the two of you can discuss the letter. I also suggest you seek counseling. It would probably help to sit down with your pastor or a counselor to discuss your differences and work on some problem-solving techniques.

You also mention that you're praying your dad grows closer to the Lord so he can find happiness. Meanwhile, you're so stressed you've started smoking again. Hmmmm. Instead of dealing with your stress by smoking, maybe you oughta try working on your own relationship with Christ.

Dear Susie:

My mom and I don't get along at all. She doesn't trust me, and I can't trust her. She tells her friends everything I tell her. Once she even believed I was on pot just because someone told her they heard a rumor about that. It wasn't true, and it hurts that she believed a rumor instead of me!

I feel like I'm going to lose it soon. I hate her. I wish she would die. I know that's horrible, but it's true. I really need help. I wish I had a mom I got along with.

Unalaska, Alaska

Wow! I'm really sorry there's such a barrier between you and your mom. I understand you're hurting because she believed a rumor over *you,* so let's go on a quick search together, okay?

Is there a reason she's having difficulty trusting you? Have you come in past your curfew? Argued for later nights? Procrastinated on your chores or promised to do something then simply forgot or got busy with something else and never did it?

These are things in moms' minds that spell *irresponsibility.* You want your mom to trust you? *Be dependable.* Prove to her you *can* be trusted.

If you haven't broken curfew or given your mom a reason to doubt you, then tell her how much you desperately want your relationship to improve. Can you suggest that you both seek counseling together? Or would she be open to both of you talking with your pastor?

The thing that concerns me is the fact that you feel hatred toward your mom. Bottom line: You must forgive even those who hurt you. You gotta learn to love and forgive. (Hint: You can't do it in your own power. Total commitment to the lordship of Christ is the key. The Holy Spirit will provide what you lack.)

Dear Susie:

My mom and dad got divorced about five years ago when I was seven. My dad remarried, and he and his wife are moving soon. They've told me to decide to either come with them or stay with my real mom.

If I go with my dad, I'll never see my mom and my brother again. If I stay with my mom, I'll never see my sister, dad, stepmom, or other brother again.

I asked if I could do the "six-month-split," but the answer was no. I would go with my dad for sure, but my mom and I are really close. But my brother (who's moving with my dad) and I are really close too.

I don't think I can live without either one of them, but whatever advice you give me, I'll take.

Phoenix, Arizona

You're in a very tough spot. And I deeply appreciate your desire to maintain family unity. It sounds like you really know and appreciate the high value God wants us to place on our families.

Let's chat for a second about the term *never*. I know it *seems* like never . . . but *nothing* is truly never except eternity (which never ends). So, can you try not to think in terms of *never?* It's not that you'll never get to see the other parent again, because in only six years you'll be eighteen and will be able to make choices to see the important people in your life.

Even though this is an extremely difficult decision (that you shouldn't have to make), I encourage you to consider staying with your mom during your adolescent years. *But* please have a heart-to-heart talk with her and try to reach a compromise. This is what I suggest:

- Remind her of how important your other family members are to you.

- Tell her you'd like to keep the lines of communication open with your brother and your dad.
- Ask if she'll consider giving you an hour or half an hour a week for long-distance calls.
- Send a picture of yourself to your brother every month. This keeps the contact fresh and keeps your face in front of him.
- When you're fifteen, you'll be able to get a job and save some money. Set definite goals for visiting: spring break, summer vacation, part of Christmas. Let your mom know up front what your goals are.

Again, try to replace your *never* thinking with *a definite visit* thinking. Keep in touch with me. You can write me at the address at the end of the book and let me know how I can continue to pray for you.

Dear Susie:
My parents make me wash dishes and empty the trash, and they don't do anything! I think this is totally unfair. What should I do?

Corpus Christi, Texas

Hold on a minute, and let's think through this a bit more. Who cooked the meal that was placed on the dishes you washed? Who bought the food? Who works a full-time job to pay for the food? *Your parents.*

Most parents assign chores to their children. Is this so they won't have to do the work? No, because a family is a unit, a team. And a team *shares* the responsibilities. Dividing the workload among family members creates a bonding, gets the work done, and establishes discipline.

Not a fun answer, huh?

I suggest you cut your parents some slack and start thinking about stuff like job stress, financial obligations, insurance, and car repairs. Then count your blessings and tell your folks how much you love and appreciate them.

Dear Susie:

My parents won't let me have a muscle shirt, and I really want one. Most of my friends have one. It's not like people don't know I wear a bra.

Walsh, Colorado

Have you asked your parents (or tried to figure out on your own) *why* they don't want you to have a muscle shirt? I'm guessing it's because your folks think they're immodest. And before you start defending this trend, just think about it for a sec. The gaping, huge armholes and low, wide necks leave nothing to the imagination.

Many times, when someone *wants* others to see her bra under what she's wearing, it's because she desires attention and wants to show off what she has.

Come on! Don't settle for that. Here's the *truth:* Guys don't want to see your bra, your slip, or your underwear. They'd much rather use their imagination than simply see everything you have to offer. Can I be even more blunt? Showcasing your underwear is cheap. It looks trashy.

I get so many letters from girls who just can't figure out why guys are always putting the moves on them. "Why can't I go out with a guy who will treat me with respect and sincerely care about *me,* instead of what he can *get* out of me?" they ask.

Well, a lot of it depends on how you dress! You want a guy to treat you like a lady? Then why are you begging your parents to let you wear muscle shirts? *What's wrong with this picture?* Wake up and stop being so willing to show the public those pieces of clothing that should never become public!

88

GUY BREAK!

Dear Susie:
I'm sixteen years old, and I've never had a boyfriend. Is there something wrong with me?

Omaha, Nebraska

It makes me sad that you think not having a boyfriend by a certain age makes you abnormal. I'd love for us to share a pepperoni-with-extra-pepperoni pizza so I could convince you that your self-worth, your fulfillment, your security, and your confidence must come from your relationship with God—*not a boy!*

Two things wrong with that: You're in another state—and *I* can't do the convincing. Wish I could. It'd be a lot easier to just force you to believe all that, but it has to come from *your* end.

It probably seems that everywhere you look you're faced with couples: TV, school, magazines . . . even youth group. This naturally makes you want to be a part of a couple also. Nothing wrong with that feeling. But there's also nothing wrong with *you!*

Guess what? God wants your happiness and fulfillment *even more than you do!* And his timing is *sooo* perfect. He's never early, yet never late.

I love the way the Old Testament prophet Habakkuk put it: "These things I plan won't happen right away. Slowly, steadily, surely, the time approaches when the vision will be fulfilled. If it seems slow, do not despair, for these things will surely come to pass. Just be patient! They will not be overdue a single day!" (2:3).

Dear Susie:
My friend is dating a boy with a bad reputation. When I expressed my concern for the situation, she said, "That's

your opinion." I'm afraid she'll cross sexual boundaries with him. How can I help her?

Waikiki, Hawaii

You sound like a terrific friend. I admire your concern for your friend. I wish she were responding differently, but it sounds like you really *want* to help. I think it's important that you let her know your apprehension about the relationship she's involved in, and it sounds like you've tried to do that.

Since she's reacting in a defensive way, wait a while and try again—but this time take extra caution to try to voice your concern in a manner and place in which she'll be less defensive.

That may be while you're shopping, out for a Coke, or spending the night at her house—whatever environment is most comfortable for the both of you. Remind her how much you value her friendship, and tell her you're glad she's excited about being in a relationship. Admit that you might be overreacting about the whole thing, but tell her you really want her to have terrific relationships with guys. So ask if the two of you can meet on a regular basis (like weekly) to talk and pray about this specific relationship she's in now.

This should prove to her that you care, and at the same time it will give her some needed accountability. It's important that you not come across as being judgmental.

If it seems appropriate, *gently* restate your concern about her boyfriend and her reputation. Remind her that sometimes it's so easy to get carried away with the excitement of just having a boyfriend that we forget about other important matters.

If she's not angry or defensive, ask if the two of you can pray before you leave.

8

A LITTLE BIT
OF EVERYTHING

Dear Susie:
 I really want to become a television actress. I take classes at a local theater. Other than this, do you have any ideas of how to break into the business?

San Diego, California

You're off to a great start! I suggest you also get involved in your school's productions. Get as much experience as possible. When I interviewed TV's *Full House* actress Candace Cameron for *Brio* magazine, she added the following advice:

- Secure an agent, and send in your picture and resumé. You can contact the Screen Actors Guild in Hollywood for a listing of available agents. It can be tough to actually get an agent. They each receive hundreds of photos and resumés! But if one of them likes your look or sees potential in you, he or she will call you to audition for an available part.
- Wait.
- If you don't live near a major agent-oriented city (such as Los Angeles, New York, Chicago, Orlando,

Washington, D.C., or Atlanta), your chances are pretty slim. Since you have to be available for auditions, it's imperative that you live close by.

Dear Susie:

On an episode of *Family Matters,* Jaleel White (Steve Urkel) said he had accepted the Lord into his heart. He then went on to say that he believed in God even though he couldn't touch, see, or hear him. This was the focus of the entire program.

Is he a new Christian? What about the rest of the cast?

Wakarusa, Indiana

Just because someone says something in a TV comedy doesn't mean he personally believes it. That's what *acting* is all about—trying to get the audience to assume the character and the actor are the same person and possess the same beliefs.

An actor merely relies on lines from a script . . . a far cry from proclaiming personal faith.

Jaleel has not made any public declaration of religious faith. When actors, musicians, athletes, or other celebrities become Christians, they usually share their faith in a public manner.

Is *anyone* on the cast a Christian? Yes. Darius McCrary (Eddie Winslow) talks very openly about what God is doing in his life.

Bottom line: Though there are many *good* people in the spotlight, being *good* doesn't make them a Christian. Don't believe everything you see. Wait until you hear an actor speak personally, instead of delivering someone else's written material.

Dear Susie:

I'm taking dance lessons, and our dance class is supposed to dance in front of our town, my school, and others in an upcoming recital. I hate the way I look in my dance costume because it's tight and skimpy.

My parents are paying a lot of money for my lessons and my costume. They've already paid for everything, but I don't want my friends or the town seeing me dressed like this. I especially don't want to dance at my school; my mom says I've already made the commitment, but the decision is up to me. What should I do?

Turlock, California

You're in a tough situation, and I feel for you. I sense you're wanting to honor your parents and please God, but to do that goes against your comfort zone in this particular situation.

Try this: Create a very specific list of pros and cons (I'm talking extensive here), sit down with your mom, and go through it *together*. Stress your desire to please your folks, but also emphasize your insecurity about your costume. Hopefully, the two of you can reach a decision you're both comfortable with.

Dear Susie:

Is it true that if you don't answer a chain letter you'll have bad luck? I've received several chain letters this year but threw them all away.

Marshfield, Wisconsin

Congrats! You did the right thing. It's silly to think a piece of paper can control your destiny. Absolutely *no one* and *nothing* has the power to govern our future except God.

Dear Susie:

My problem is Luke Perry of TV's *Beverly Hills 90210*. I'm really addicted to the show, and every time I see him it's like falling in love.

93

I think of him maybe every minute. My grades are even suffering. How can I unhook myself?

San Francisco, California

I don't think you can really be "in love" with someone you haven't even met. You can, however, be infatuated. *I* think that you're simply caught up in Luke's TV character, Dillan McKay, whom you probably view as cool, exciting, and romantic.

Luke Perry, on the other hand, uses so much foul language in his interviews that he has to be bleeped or chopped up to get rid of all the garbage.

How can you "unhook" yourself from Luke? Simple: Quit watching *90210*.

Dear Susie:

I have a great life, but I'm depressed. I have terrific friends, good grades, and an awesome relationship with God. I also have a very caring family that I love very much.

I don't know why I'm depressed. I was depressed before my hamster died. He lived one year and seven months. What do you think about all this? What should I do?

Madison, Virginia

It sounds like your life is basically going pretty well, with the exception of this one area. I realize this started

94

before your hamster died . . . but before we go any further, let's talk about that.

We can love our pets so much that they become like a best friend or even a family member to us. (I sure count my golden retriever, Jamaica Jane, as one of my best friends.) When they die, we experience a deep sense of grief and loss.

Even though your blues began before this loss, it *could* be that the death of your hamster has intensified your depression.

It's also important to realize that your body is going through a tremendous amount of change right now. Your hormones are waking up and basically going wacko. (Sounds scary, but this is a *normal* part of being a teen.) Whenever our hormones fluctuate, our emotions go up and down.

So, what's the answer? Sounds like you have a fantastic family! Can you share this with your mom? Chances are she has experienced the same thing.

Your pastor, your grandma, a Christian counselor, or your youth minister would also be good people to talk with. Why talk with someone? Because you need help identifying the source of depression. Once that's identified, you can deal with it and get on with your life.

Dear Susie:

I am so desperate to get a snake! I've never held one, but I know I would like to. My mom is absolutely against this and won't let me get one. I thought maybe you could give me some advice on how to talk her into it.

Seattle, Washington

Since you've never held a snake, what makes you so sure you'd really like it? Ask your mom if the two of you can just "check it out" first. After talking with a pet store owner and seeing a snake up close, you may decide that's not really what you want after all.

If you still want a snake and your mom is still against the idea, ask her if you can raise earthworms. The money's good, and when handling them you can just pretend they're a hundred pounds heavier.

Dear Susie:
I *love* to write stories, articles, poetry . . . anything! Some of my stuff is pretty good, and I'd like to get it published. Can you give me some suggestions?

Harrisburg, Nebraska

Are you familiar with the *Writer's Market?* This is a book published each year that contains every publisher in America: book publishers, magazines, videos . . . even greeting cards!

Under each publisher, you'll find valuable information—like how much they pay, if they accept freelance material (anytime you send something to a publisher without being asked, it's considered freelance), what kind of circulation they have, and much more.

You'll also find several different sections in the *Writer's Market* that highlight special kinds of publications: teen, religious, sports, educational, etc.

Check out a copy at your local library . . . or purchase one from a nearby bookstore for approximately twenty-five dollars. *But first* ask your English teacher to read your stuff and offer an honest evaluation. Her input will help you polish your material before sending it to a publisher.

Dear Susie:
I'm twelve years old and want to see R-rated movies, but my mom won't let me. When do you think I should be able to see them?

Wyandotte, Michigan

When do you think Jesus would be comfortable sitting with you while you're watching an R-rated movie? There's your answer.

Dear Susie:

In our school, I'm one of two trombonists. The other day I overheard the other player say I was hopeless. Now I'm wondering if I should quit or keep playing in band?

Willowdale, Ontario, Canada

Don't get discouraged just because one tooter is too tight to be nice. Maybe he or she is better than you right now ... but here's the tickler: there's always this summer! While he's swimming, camping, and forgetting to practice, you can surge ahead by tooting till you're tired of your tunes. Then guess who'll be trailing behind?

Dear Susie:

I've been really depressed for a long time. Life seems boring, tasteless, and monotonous. Nothing interests me anymore: boys, friends, family . . . even God. Everything has lost its magic touch for me. I also worry a lot about school, driver's ed (not passing), and that my friends suddenly won't like me anymore.

I always think about things like death, war, and poverty.

Basically, the only time I feel happy is when I'm watching a movie or reading a book, because it's like putting aside my problems and entering a different world.

Is this normal? Will I ever be the carefree, happy person I used to be?

Grand Rapids, Michigan

No, it's not normal. But let's just chat for a few seconds before I suggest you talk with someone, okay?

Depression is a word that's being tossed around a lot. Teens often say things like "Dad won't let me use the car. I'm *sooo* depressed"; or "We have so much homework in this class. I've been depressed for a week!"

Depression has several definitions, but let's go with something simple—like the fact that your feelings seem frozen inside of you. You seem stuck. Think about your feelings. What are they? Fear? Anger? Guilt?

Identify the feeling that's stuck, then ask yourself *why* you're experiencing that particular emotion. For example, I'm feeling angry. *At what or whom?* My boyfriend. *Why?* He physically abuses me.

NOW it's understandable why you're feeling so angry. But how do you deal with this anger? You're *not* dealing with it. You're stuck. Trying to cover up a feeling you don't want to look at can get pretty exhausting. And guess what? You can't just cover up *one* feeling. You have to hide *all* of them—even the good ones (like joy, love, concern, etc.). That's depression.

Everyone has feelings. Sometimes they're too big to deal with. We have a choice: Either shove them down inside, or talk with someone. While sharing with another individual will not always solve the problem, it *will* make a difference!

My suggestion? Choose an adult whom you trust, and share this with him or her. Your parents, pastor, youth minister, or school counselor are all good people to consider.

Will you also take a quick look at the following questions? Maybe they'll help you zero in on some answers as well.

- What are you watching on TV?
- What type of books are you reading? (You said the only time you felt good was when you escaped through one of these two avenues, yet you are always down. Our feelings are impacted by what we take in.)
- Are you getting any exercise? (Our brain releases a certain chemical when we exercise, and it actually lifts our spirits.)
- What are you eating? (Our diet also has a big impact on how we feel. If you're skipping meals or chowing down on Cokes and candy bars, your emotions are definitely going to be up and down.)

Again . . . please talk with someone!

Dear Susie:
I keep telling myself that I'll clean my messy room, but I never do. How can I be motivated?
Taylor, Michigan

Don't try to clean your entire room all at once. Instead, try setting small, reasonable goals. Begin by getting everything off the floor in the morning. Take a break, and then come back and tackle the second thing on your list: hanging up your clothes. The next day you can move on to the third goal. By the end of the week your room should look good enough to have all your friends over to celebrate!

(When you're completely finished, how 'bout coming over to my office and helping me get started?)

Dear Susie:
How can I save my money for a long time without spending it?

Wenatchee, Washington

Send it to the address in the back of this book, and I'll take care of it for you! Just kidding!

Stashing the cash is never done fast! Start your savings spree by making a list of everything you spend money on for one week. Then go back and evaluate how much spending was really necessary and how much money was simply blown.

Next, decide on a figure that you're not going to blow from here on. Banks are often a good option. By controlling your yearnings, you'll advance your earnings and will probably save enough by the end of the summer to buy yourself something special.

Dear Susie:
I have this really big problem: I steal. I've never taken anything from a store—just money from my mom's purse. I've prayed about it and have tried to resist temptation, but it's not working. I really want to stop.

Bangor, Maine

I'm glad you want to stop. Since you've spent some time praying about it, I'm assuming you know it's wrong. For *anyone* involved in a habit she's trying to break, it always helps to tell someone. Why? Because that person can hold you accountable.

About a year ago, I wanted to cut down on the amount of Cokes I was drinking. I told a friend so she could hold me accountable. I knew every time I saw Shirley, she'd ask me, "How many Cokes have you had?" It helped me cut back.

If you know that a couple of times each week someone is going to be asking you if you've taken anything, chances are you'll stop stealing.

Maybe we should also chat about *why* you're stealing money from your mom's purse. Is it because you don't think you have enough? If that's the reason, ask your mom if the two of you can sit down and talk about your allowance.

Or is it simply because you want to see how much you can get away with? This is a dangerous challenge; sooner or later, it will catch up with you. You may need to seek professional counseling.

Dear Susie:

I'm a pastor's daughter, so naturally everyone thinks I'm perfect. But I'm *not!* I love country music, and people are always saying, "You're the pastor's daughter! Shouldn't you be listening to violin music?"

New Haven, Connecticut

I'm sorry you're having to deal with being stereotyped. People are placing certain expectations on you because of your dad's occupation. Truth is, you're *not* perfect— none of us are. You're normal.

Many kids in your situation have started doing things they shouldn't have (and don't necessarily even *want* to do—drinking, drugs, sex, bad language) just to prove to those around them that they're not perfect.

I don't sense that kind of rebellion from your letter. I admire the respect you obviously have for your parents, and the love you have for Jesus that keeps you from feeling you have to prove anything to anyone.

Be patient with those who are stereotyping you. This is a teaching situation—an opportunity for you to help them learn that you can be a pastor's daughter, be right with God, yet have many different interests.

Dear Susie:

Within the last four years both of my grandfathers, a great aunt, and great uncle have died. At first, I thought

101

about how I'd never see them again. But recently I've realized that I *will* see them again in heaven. I know they're much better off with God.

When my relatives get together and start remembering them, they cry. I try to tell them what I just told you, but they look at me like I'm crazy. They say something like, "Kids these days just don't have any respect."

Am I wrong to feel glad that they're better off? Sure, I miss them. I'm *not glad* they're dead, but I *am* grateful they're not suffering anymore.

Oregon, Illinois

People react to tragedy in different ways. Your way of coping with loss may not be the same as another person's. That's okay. Everyone has to deal with loss in a way that's most comfortable for them.

Some people find it easier to mourn for a long time. Others mourn briefly, then focus on all the positive attributes of their deceased loved one. Neither is wrong.

Like you, I'm glad your grandfathers and great aunt and uncle aren't suffering anymore. Your relatives who are still mourning their passing are also glad, but they just may need a little more time to grieve.

Let them grieve. When you're together, continue to share the positive memories you have of your grandfathers and aunt and uncle, but don't try to force them out of grief. Let God and time be the healing factors in their pain.

Dear Susie:

I'm sixteen and have been a Christian for nine years. I have a good relationship with Christ and am very active in my youth group.

My problem is that everyone I'm close to is pro-life, and most people consider *me* to be pro-life also.

Honestly, I don't know what I am. Both sides have very

convincing arguments. Who do I believe? Who is telling the truth?

Providence, Rhode Island

I appreciate your desire for truth. If we just look at scientific facts, we can see logically that life begins at conception. From the moment an egg is fertilized by a sperm, a living human being is created.

Just a few weeks later, the unborn baby even has its own heartbeat! It also has brain waves that can be detected and it can feel pain. Knowing this, is it really hard to believe this is actually a life?

My doctor gives the following example: A Christian attorney recently pointed out that an unborn baby has the legal right to inherit a portion of the father's estate if he should die before the baby is born. However, in most states, the baby's mother can choose to end his or her life up until the time of delivery. In other words, the laws of our land give the unborn clear *property* rights, but not *human* rights! This is insane.

Those are simply logical, proven facts. But let's also take a look at what God has to say.

> You made all the delicate, inner parts of my body, and knit them together in my mother's womb. Thank you for making me so wonderfully complex! It is amazing to think about. Your workmanship is marvelous—and how well I know it. You were there while I was being formed in utter seclusion! You saw me before I was born and scheduled each day of my life before I began to breathe. Every day was recorded in your Book!
>
> How precious it is, Lord, to realize that you are thinking about me constantly! I can't even count how many times a day your thoughts turn towards me. And when I waken in the morning, you are still thinking of me!
>
> Psalm 139:13–18

That pretty much says it all, doesn't it?

Dear Susie:

I feel like a lazy lump! I've tried softball, soccer, volleyball, and basketball but nothing works. I have absolutely no sports coordination whatsoever.

I want to be interested in what we do in gym, but I just don't have any confidence. I've already prayed about it. Can you help?

Sussex, Delaware

We're confident in the things we do well. You may not be good at the sports you mentioned, but I'll bet there are tons of other things you're great at! And it's my guess that in *those* areas you *are* confident.

Not everyone is cut out to be an athlete. Don't beat yourself up over things you're not doing well. If you really want to work on developing coordination, though, here are a few other ideas that can help accomplish that.

Aerobics. Rent a video or exercise to an aerobics show on television. There are plenty around. You can do this alone (so you won't be embarrassed), and develop muscle coordination at the same time.

Swimming. This sport actually works almost every muscle in your body. It's a terrific way to tone *and* develop some skill.

Bicycling. Wanna develop endurance? This will do the trick while defining your legs at the same time.

Skating. If you don't own a pair of skates, consider using your local rink twice a month. You'll develop agility *and* coordination.

Meanwhile, concentrate on all the other things you *can* do well!

Dear Susie:
I like to wear tight stretch pants with big, oversized tops. Some people say this is immodest, and that I shouldn't dress like this. I'm not overweight, and *I* think they look good.

Gaithersburg, Maryland

Know who the best judge will be? Your mom. Ask her opinion, and if she says they don't look good on you, she's probably right.

Dear Susie:
I heard that Liz Claiborne gives 40 percent of her profits to the Church of Satan. Is this true?

Chicago, Illinois

The actual rumor that's been floating around is that Liz Claiborne *publicly* said this on the *Oprah Winfrey Show.* But guess what? Liz was never even on Oprah's show! She was, however, on *A.M. Chicago* back in 1983, which later evolved into the *Oprah Winfrey Show.*

According to the transcript, there was never any mention of how she spent her money. The reps from Channel 7 in Chicago also confirm this. Liz Claiborne's company representative says Liz occasionally attends an Episcopalian church and sometimes donates money to wildlife foundations.

So why the rumor? Who knows? A few years ago similar rumors were spread about Procter & Gamble and even McDonald's. They turned out to be false. From all I can tell, the Liz Claiborne rumor is also false.

Dear Susie:
 Does the Bible talk about rock music?

Rankin, Mississippi

Well, back in the days when David tended sheep, he sometimes brought his portable harp with him. While the sheep grazed, he'd often climb up on a rock, sit down, and make music. I *guess* we could call that rock music . . . *tee hee.*

Other than that, no. Madonna, Red Hot Chili Peppers, Janet, Expose, and Michael Bolton are never mentioned. But even though the Bible never mentions rock music

specifically, it does offer guidelines about what we listen to or watch. Check out my response to the letter on page 27 about movies.

Dear Susie:

I believe God has given us this earth to take care of, and I support the efforts of those who want to save it. But recently, our Sunday school teacher said it wasn't worth saving. He went on to say that we'd be leaving soon because of the rapture, and after that it would soon be destroyed.

Now I'm confused and don't know what to believe.

Jacksonville, Florida

No one knows when the rapture will occur. So in the meantime, while we're waiting, it makes sense to do all we can to preserve the planet we live on; just don't become a fanatic about it. Saving the earth, trees, or animals is not as important as people are.

Many activists equate their cause with human life. For instance, I'm all for protecting animals, but the bottom line is they are *not* equal to humans, therefore, they should not have equal rights. Yes, let's work to protect them (and the earth and a million other things), but let's keep it all in perspective.

People are—and always will be—the most important thing around.

Dear Susie:

Are you married, and do you have any kids?

Waukegan, Illinois

I'm still single, and I don't have any kids. *But* I have the best golden retriever in the world (Jamaica Jane), who can balance an ice cube on her nose, toss it in the air, and catch it in her mouth. She can also

get my news-
paper and my
mail . . . and
unfortunately,
the neighbor's
newspaper and
the neighbor's
mail. Her latest
adventure? I'm
teaching her
how to open
the refrigerator.

I also have
three good-
looking
nephews: Scott,
Brett, and Matt
Shellenberger,
who live in Oklahoma
City.

Dear Susie:

I still sleep with a night-light, and I'm in the seventh grade. What's wrong with me?

Hamilton, Michigan

You're not alone! *Lots* of people sleep with a night-light. My parents use night-lights throughout their house simply because it helps them see where they're going when they have to get up during the night.

It's certainly okay to sleep with a night-light; there's absolutely nothing wrong with that. If you're wanting to stop, though, ask yourself *why* you sleep with one.

Is it because you need to see your way around in the middle of the night? Or is it because you're frightened? We're usually scared when we don't feel safe. Are there reasons you don't feel safe? Has something happened to make you uncomfortable at night?

Answering these questions will give you some insight on why you're using a night-light. You might also want to think of other things you can do to feel safe at night. For instance, you could sleep with your favorite stuffed animal instead of using a night-light. Or you could ask your parents to help you put a lock on your door. What about letting your pet sleep in the room at night with you?

Any of these ideas will give you a good start in giving up your night-light . . . but more important than turning off your night-light is trying to figure out why you're using one when you don't want to. Dare to ask yourself the needed questions, then recruit your parents' help in doing something about it.

Dear Susie:
Is it true that girls are lonelier than boys?

Perkins, South Dakota

Well, yes and no. It's true that females have more need for connectedness, and they express it more. This means they usually work harder at establishing several friendships, and they pour themselves into their friends. Women are often more in touch with their feelings and openly share them.

Guys also need friends, but society seems to say that boys aren't supposed to have any kind of intimacy with each other. So while girls tend to share *everything* (grades, secrets, who they like, makeup, clothes, and FEELINGS), guys tend to focus more on events—yesterday's game, the fight in the locker room, anything gross from the school cafeteria. When we focus on *feelings,* we naturally develop more intimacy than by simply sharing about *happenings*. The result? Girls often

109

have closer, more intimate friends they can cry or laugh with, while guys have a few friends they shoot hoops with and talk about girls with.

Dear Susie:
I hear a lot about flirting, but what exactly is it? And how do you do it?

Fountain Valley, California

Flirting is simply trying to get a guy's attention. This can be done in a variety of ways—even saying hi to a guy you like can be considered flirting.

There's good flirting and bad flirting. Good flirting is getting a guy's attention through safe and acceptable ways, like having a conversation with him, smiling at him, or laughing at his jokes. Nothing wrong with this. It's a natural part of growing up and learning how to establish friendships with the opposite sex.

Bad flirting is trying to sexually arouse a guy, and *that* can get you into a lot of trouble.

Dear Susie:
A friend of mine told me that Esprit gives 50 percent of their sales to abortions. Is this true?

Saskatoon, Saskatchewan, Canada

Esprit *is* pro-choice, but I don't have figures on how much they donate to this cause. I do know that last year they sponsored a national poster contest in which teen girls were encouraged to support abortion through creating posters for a competition. The posters were hung in stores that sold Esprit clothing and were also printed in several teen magazines.

110

GUY BREAK!

Dear Susie:

What do guys do at slumber parties?

Guys don't have slumber parties. Occasionally, two or three guys will spend the night together, but it's nothing like the fifteen-guest slumber parties girls throw.

When they do camp out at a friend's house, they do some of the same things girls do: eat pizza, watch videos, scarf some chips, call the opposite sex on the phone, down some ice cream, talk about the opposite sex, eat brownies, scheme to wrap toilet paper around someone's front yard, and eat pizza again.

Dear Susie:

Why do some girls fall for rebels? I don't smoke or cuss, and I obey my parents (most of the time). But I do seem to be attracted to guys who are rebels.

Oak Grove, Kentucky

I admire you for not smoking or cussing—especially when there's so much pressure in the "blackboard jungle" to do so. There could be several reasons why you're attracted to rebellious guys.

Since you really haven't rebelled against your parents, I'm guessing you like to please them. You want to make them happy, but there could be a *part* of you that really wants to rebel. By liking guys you know they wouldn't approve of, this is an avenue of rebellion.

Also, there may be a part of you that's a rescuer—someone who needs to feel needed. When you see a guy who's always getting into trouble and breaking the rules, you see someone who "needs" your help.

111

Guess what? It's not your job to be a rescuer. Your job is to develop a more open relationship with your parents. If you're feeling a need to rebel, maybe you're holding some frustration inside. *Talk* with your mom and dad about it.

BEFORE READING
any further, do one of the following . . .

- Memorize Ephesians 3:20 (my favorite verse).
- Change your sheets.
- Write a song.
- Create a slogan that promotes clean teeth.
- Pray for your pastor's wife.
- Think of a new way to comb your hair.
- Pretend you're six years old again and blow bubbles.
- Write a letter to Chris Castile from TV's *Step by Step*. (He's a Christian and would love to hear from you. Tell him "Susie said you love Skittles candy.") Chris Castile, Step by Step, ABC-TV, 2040 Avenue of the Stars, Century City, CA 90067.

9

ALL IN THE FAMILY

Dear Susie:
My mom and sisters keep hurting my feelings by making fun of me. What should I do?

Portland, Oregon

Ouch! Being made fun of can really cut deeply, can't it? Your letter is pretty short; I wish I had more details—like *what* exactly they're doing and saying.

Could it be that they don't mean to hurt your feelings? Many times people hurt us without meaning to. For them it's just harmless teasing, but to us it's much more.

I don't see any way around this without talking with them. They need to know you're hurting. It may be too hard for you to verbalize what you're feeling, so I suggest writing a letter. Include everything you can think of.

Then hold on to it for a week. Read over it a few times. Pray about it. Think on it. Then ask your mom and sisters for a convenient time you can get together. When that time arrives, explain there are some things you want to talk with them about that you've written on paper. Give each of them a copy and wait for their response. Hopefully, this will create some open lines of communication for you to draw closer together.

Dear Susie:

My brother is a senior and very talented. He's a good-looking guy with a great personality. What I don't understand is, why he's so shy around girls.

He told me that if a girl turned him down, he'd feel crushed for weeks. My mom has been praying for him to have more self-confidence, but is there something *I* can do too?

Owensboro, Kentucky

I admire your concern. The fact that you *want* to help really speaks highly of you. Your bro is lucky to have such a terrific sis! Make a point to affirm and encourage him in the things he does well.

Also, watch for opportunities to compliment him in other areas as well. For instance, does he look great in his blue sweater? Tell him! Do you appreciate it when he opens a door for you? Let him know how special that makes you feel. Did he do well in something at school? Give him a fun card, and let him know how proud of him you are. And whenever you hear someone *else* compliment him, be sure to pass it on. Make him aware of the good things others are saying about him.

It may take awhile, but eventually your bro will not only *listen* to what's happening around him, but he will begin *believing* it as well.

Dear Susie:

My sister is Miss Popularity and has about a zillion friends. All the boys—including the ones I like—kiss the ground she walks on. I really don't want to be jealous of her, but I guess I am. Please help!

Webster, West Virginia

Wow! Thanks so much for your honesty. Facing up to jealousy isn't easy, but admitting it is the first step in

dealing with it. How do you handle jealousy? How are you dealing with it? Are you ignoring her? Being mean to her? Trying to find different friends?

You've admitted you're jealous of her, now take responsibility for that and decide to deal with it in a positive way. How? I suggest you concentrate on all *your* strengths—things you do well and positive characteristics you have in comparison with your sister.

Be happy about her gifts, then find ways with your own personality that you can make more friends. You're dealing with a heavy issue. You're off to a good start, and you might work through it on your own . . . but I suggest you talk with an adult—your mom or youth leader.

Also, use this confusing time to dig into God's Word for guidance in handling jealousy. Grab a special notebook—let's call it your spiritual growth book—and record your thoughts and concerns about this in it. THIS is how we grow spiritually—by giving God the hard times we encounter and allowing him to teach us, reshape us, and guide us through them.

I'm listing a few Scriptures to get you started. I suggest you read each verse, then paraphrase it (put it in your words) in your spiritual growth book. Also, try writing your struggle about this in a prayer and keep that in your notebook too. Place a check mark by each Scripture after you've read it and recorded your response to it in your notebook.

☐ Psalm 139

☐ Isaiah 43:1–2

☐ 2 Corinthians 12:20

☐ Galatians 5:19–24

Dear Susie:
Lately I've been spending more time with my friends than with my family. When I don't want to do something with them, they feel like I don't care enough about our family.

I don't want to turn into the average pathetic teenager, but I also want to have fun with my friends. What do I do?

Chittenden, Vermont

What you're experiencing is a normal part of growing up. Try telling your parents just what you told me. Remind them how much you love and value them, and ask if you can help create a "family night." This would be a special night each week (or every *other* week) that your family will set aside to do something together.

It might be bowling, playing mini-golf, going out for pizza, or renting some classic videos and munching on popcorn. The point is, it doesn't have to be elaborate—just something you all enjoy. This will guarantee cherished time together and also allow you to spend some other nights with your friends.

The important thing? Once you decide on a specific night for "family night," *stick with it.* Your parents need to see that you value their fellowship enough to keep your end of the deal.

118

Dear Susie:

I have a cute new baby sister. But sometimes I feel left out—especially when she starts crying.

West Branch, Michigan

You're suddenly having to share all the attention *you* used to get from your parents with someone else. That's tough. It's hard because you're having to adjust to something that's producing uncomfortable feelings in you. It's normal to feel left out. It's natural to feel lonely . . . but it still hurts, doesn't it?

It's my guess that you want to work through this as quickly as possible, right? Well, on your own it's going to take longer. If you'll share your feelings with your parents, though, they can probably help you through the process.

Explain how excited you are to have an addition to the family but that *you* still need attention too. Tell them you want to be involved with the baby (yes, that means not just playing with her, but helping care for her too!) and still need to be needed.

Your parents will probably welcome your honesty and openness because they've probably been thinking about your adjustment even longer than you have! Talk with them.

119

Dear Susie:
My friend hates my brother and is constantly telling me. I *love* him. How should I handle this?

Pepeekeo, Hawaii

The first question that pops into my mind is, Why is she doing this? Could she be taking any clues from *you?* Have you ever complained about your brother or bad-mouthed him in front of her? If so, she's probably unaware of your deep love for him.

Many times among brothers and sisters a weird sense of loyalty exists. I say *weird* because this particular attitude says, "Okay, maybe *I* ream on my bro a lot, but nobody else better!"

In other words, *you* have the right to tear him down because he's in your family, but if anyone dares to agree with you, the loyalty kicks in and you defend him.

That's not genuine love. And maybe this isn't the case with you. I'm having to do some guesswork from your short letter. So let me just challenge you to give yourself a quick little mind search. If you *are* guilty of this, apologize to your friend for cutting your brother down in front of her, then tell her how much you love him.

If you *haven't* ragged on him to your friend, and she's downing him for no apparent reason—other than the fact that she just doesn't like him—gently, but firmly tell her she's hurting your feelings. Try something like this: "I'm glad we're friends, but it makes me question just how deep our friendship really is when you make such negative comments about my brother. I love him. He's my family. It hurts to hear you talk about him that way. So please quit, okay?"

If she refuses to change her behavior? Find a *real* friend—one who will love you *and* your family.

Dear Susie:

About a month ago I wrote my brother a note telling him I wanted us to be closer—but he thought I didn't mean it. I'm thirteen and he's fifteen. I love him a lot and want to be his friend, but I get nervous when I try to talk with him. How can I get over this?

Overland Park, Kansas

We're dealing with a few unanswered questions here. First, how do you know he thought you didn't mean it? Are you sure he even got the letter? And how do you know he read it?

And, yes, maybe he did get the letter but feels insecure about showing his feelings. If this is the case, it may be just as hard for *him* to approach *you.*

I suggest you talk with one of your parents about all this. Share your feelings with them—not accusations. Maybe they can help you feel secure enough to approach him.

I'm glad you want to develop a close relationship with your brother, but like any relationship, it will take some work. Consider writing him another letter. Tell him again how much you love him and want to get to know him better. Then wait a few days and ask him if he got the letter and what he thought about it.

Dear Susie:

My older sister and I have begun to develop a close relationship, and I love it! But lately, she's been lying to our parents about where she's going and whom she's going with. I want to tell my parents but don't want to ruin our new, close relationship. What do I do?

Hartford, Connecticut

I think you need to begin by being honest with your sister. Tell her how much you love and value your relation-

121

ship with her but that there's something turning inside of you that doesn't feel good. And that *something* is the lie that's going on. No one should expect that of you. We just can't compromise our values and feel good about it—ever! You'll continue to live in turmoil until you straighten out this mess. Again, start by telling your sis how you feel.

Then tell her you're giving *her* the opportunity to come clean with your folks. Give her a two-week time limit. Let her know that if she doesn't talk by then, you will.

If your sister gets angry and withdraws from you, then it's obvious that she's only been using you. That's not real love. Continue to love her without condoning lies and breaking your parents' rules.

Dear Susie:

My Christian cousin and I have been close friends for a long time, and we do a lot of things together. Lately he's been acting different—opening doors for me and inviting me to a lot of his family's activities.

On July 4, while watching some public fireworks with his brothers and sisters, he reached for my hand . . . and I let him hold it. Now I feel guilty. After all, he *is* my cousin. What should I do?

La Junta, Colorado

I know you're confused, but it sounds like you're actually more in touch with your feelings than you realize—and that's great. You know you enjoy being with your cousin and you like his company, but you're confused because of the feelings you experience when he holds your hand.

It's *normal* to feel tingly and special when a guy we like holds our hand. The factor that's making you feel guilty is knowing you're related. Using your conscience as a guide is a wise thing to do—and it sounds like your conscience is trying to tell you something.

122

You didn't mention how old you are, but I'm guessing you're both close to the same age and are both at the stage of beginning to like and notice the opposite sex. Without talking with him about this, you can only guess what's going on in his mind. Was he just reaching for your hand as an expression? A simple demonstration that he enjoys being with you? Maybe. But probably not.

I imagine a little more was going through his mind . . . and you have a right to feel uncomfortable. I understand your closeness and know you don't want to jeopardize that, but I'm encouraging you to listen to your conscience. When we feel guilty about *anything,* it's a good sign to end whatever we're involved in.

Try talking with him in a comfortable, relaxed atmosphere. Tell him how proud you are to be his cousin, and how glad you are that you're in the same family. Let him know that you'll always cherish the closeness the two of you share, and tell him you would *never* want anything to damage that; therefore, you cannot see him in any way (like a boyfriend) except as your cousin and forever friend.

Dear Susie:
   How can I get along with my sister better? I want to be a "peacemaker," but all we do is fight.

Ouiedo, Florida

Try choosing a specific time and place each night to pray for her, and let her know about your decision. For example, you might tell her something like this, "I really care about you and want us to be a lot closer. I hate fighting, and I'm sorry for the times I get angry. But from now on, every night, I'm going to be right here at the couch in the living room praying for us. If you want to join me, that would be great! But if not, that's okay. When you see me here, you'll know what I'm doing and why I'm doing it."

I wonder how your relationship will be affected when she sees you praying for *her* for two months? Four months? Six months? I believe God will honor that kind of commitment. But the key? *Consistency.* Don't dare make this kind of statement if you're not going to follow through. If you're afraid you won't be able to do this every night, then set a different standard: two nights a week, or every Sunday night. You know your schedule. Try it!

Dear Susie:

I'm eleven years old, and my fourteen-year-old sister is embarrassed to have me around. I'm mature for my age (my parents and sister can testify to that), but it still doesn't help. What can I do to help my sister not be so embarrassed?

Richmond, Virginia

Don't assume your sister's embarrassment is because of *you.* She may say that, but at fourteen years of age, a *lot* is going on with her body (inside and outside) that can make her feel insecure. Everything in her world is changing right now. Give her a little space, and let her feel her way through this growing time of her life.

You say that you're mature for your age. Do you mean physically or emotionally? If you're maturing faster *physically* than your older sister is, *that* might be making her feel uncomfortable and embarrassed around you. While there's absolutely nothing you can do to speed up or slow down your body's physical growth, make sure you never crack jokes or make sarcastic remarks about *her* body.

Compliment her when she looks good, continue to be proud of her (and let her know it), and pray for her during this tough time of growing up.

Dear Susie:

My brother is in the ninth grade, and he's been getting a lot of calls from girls. Fine, but the other day I saw him putting his arm around a girl I know.

All of his girlfriends are treating me like a sister just to get to my brother. They're taking advantage of me, and I don't like it. So, what do I do?

Raleigh, North Carolina

No one likes to feel used. It hurts. It's definitely okay not to be a part of the "user's plan." Realize that *you* have the power to make some important choices in this. *You* get to decide if you want to continue hanging around people who use you, or if you want to seek other friends who aren't interested in your brother.

Instead of taking this so personally ("They don't like me, they just want to get to my brother"), try to take a step back from what's happening and think long and hard about each person you feel is using you.

Some of these girls (when you really think hard about it) may be people you're not really interested in cultivating a friendship with. That's okay. Again, *you* get to decide.

125

But on the other hand (when you really think hard about it) you may realize others are worth investing your time in—even though they like your brother. You may come to realize that they genuinely like you too and sincerely want your friendship!

Dear Susie:
My little sister is starting to invade my privacy. My mom won't do anything about it. What's worse is that she and I have to share a bedroom. Help!

Victorville, California

How is she invading your privacy? Is she reading your diary, journal, or notes to your friends? Get a lockbox. Is she listening to your conversations during phone calls? Ask mom if you can have a specific (and reasonable) time each night to use the phone privately. Is she asking a million questions?

If so, she's simply being a typical little sister. The fact that she's asking *you* is a way of showing her admiration and confidence in you.

126

Chances are she really looks up to you. Take that as a compliment. About talking with your mom . . . you say she won't do anything about it, but how have you approached her? At the end of the day while she's trying to fix dinner? Or as a complainer? ("Mom, make her *stop!*")

Ask your mom for a time when the two of you can sit down together and talk uninterrupted—but do your part first. Make a list of the issues you feel are really important and need to be dealt with. Your sis asking questions is not really a matter of privacy—it's just bothersome to you. So don't list that.

If she's reading your private material, that's worth discussing. But beside each issue you list, include a possible solution. This will let your mom know you've put a lot of thought into what you're saying, and she won't feel the whole thing falls on her shoulders.

Dear Susie:
My older brother is fat and has a very short temper. No one likes him, and I feel sorry for him. I try to take up for him whenever possible.

I like to sit with the other teens at church, but he gets mad if *I* move or if I ask *him* to move. Sometimes I want to get away from him and just spend more time with my friends, but I feel guilty.

Minneapolis, Minnesota

There's nothing wrong with wanting to sit with your friends. Your love for your brother comes through loud and clear. I can tell you genuinely care about him . . . but you need to think about yourself too.

Try to figure out *why* you feel guilty. If it's because he doesn't have any friends, then maybe he needs to work on that short temper. NO ONE likes to be around someone who gets mad easily. That's something *he* needs to deal with—not you.

127

You can't compensate for his shortcomings; that's being an *enabler* (which is a fancy term for helping him continue with bad or negative habits).

Have you talked with your parents about this? Surely they see that he's overweight, doesn't have friends, and gets angry. Ask them to consider some professional counseling. Your bro needs to get a good handle on this *now* so he can have healthy and fulfilling relationships as an adult.

GUY BREAK!

Dear Susie:
I don't know how to get guys' attention. Should I be forward or let them come to me? There's one boy in particular I'm interested in.

Fruitvale, British Columbia, Canada

Start with something small, like just saying hi to him—calling him by name. Then, if you have a class together, ask him how he did on a recent test or inquire about a homework assignment.

If you don't have any classes together, find out what he's interested in. Does he play on the basketball team? Is he a computer whiz? Does he like music? Once you've found out what some of his hobbies are, you can use that information to begin a conversation and keep it going.

Any guy will definitely notice this. After all, *everyone* enjoys the company of someone who shows an interest in them.

Dear Susie:
Do you think that the guy should be smarter than the girl in a relationship?

St. Simons, Georgia

No. I don't think it matters who's the smartest.

10

I HAVE THIS FRIEND WHO . . .

Dear Susie:
I'm friends with a girl at school who is really depressed over this certain guy. She's even tried to commit suicide by slashing her wrists. How should I treat her? How should I act around her?

Enterprise, Alaska

I hope you can make your friend realize that suicide will cause tons more grief and problems than it supposedly solves. Point out all the great qualities you see in her, and help her focus on the fact that God has a special plan for each of his children. She *does* have an exciting future—if she'll let God be in charge.

Sometimes it's tough . . . but God wants our eyes on *him* instead of *people*. That's because he's promised *never* to leave us or fail us. People will always disappoint us, though, because we're all human.

Attempting suicide indicates very serious problems. Can you direct your friend to talk with someone who can help? A counselor may help her develop a healthier self-concept and lean on God.

Dear Susie:

I have a friend who makes fun of me and criticizes me because I don't wear makeup and I'm short. She also told me to my face that I have a man's legs (because I don't shave), and that I can't sing. How can I tell her this really hurts?

Camilla, Georgia

This is a *friend?* NOT! A *friend* doesn't criticize you behind your back *or* to your face. A *friend* affirms you, helps you believe in yourself, and stands by you. (Read 1 Corinthians 13—the definition of *genuine* friendship.)

Although shaving your legs may lessen the sarcasm for a while, it's my guess she'll find something else to rag on. Women in Europe don't shave their legs. It's not like you'll die if you don't. If you *want* to start shaving, talk with your mom and explain to her how badly you're hurting.

About makeup: *Many* women like the natural look, or because of allergies, they wear very little, if any, makeup. Nothing wrong with that! If, however, you *want* to enhance your natural beauty, don't goop up heavily; use it sensibly and talk with your mom about the two of you going to a beauty consultant at the mall for a makeup demo. This will help you learn what looks best on you.

Meanwhile, look for a new friend . . . and consistently practice being the kind of friend to others that you want for yourself.

Dear Susie:

I'm thirteen years old and one of my friends has cancer. They first found it in her stomach. She's a strong believer and didn't get sick from her first round of chemo. What can I do to cheer her up besides sending cards and visiting?

Greenup, Illinois

You sound like a TERRIFIC friend! I think what you're already doing is shouting volumes to your sick pal. Your cards and personal visits tell her that you love her and are concerned about her well-being.

Does she have other friends you could encourage to visit also? What about taking her some of your favorite videos? There are several hot Christian music videos available that she might enjoy watching (and singing with). Also, she would probably enjoy classics like *Heidi, Swiss Family Robinson,* or *The Sound of Music.*

Dear Susie:

My friend is overweight and diets but nothing seems to work. I give her hints about exercising and eating more fruits and vegetables, but she doesn't like many fruits and vegetables. I love her and don't want to be

133

as blunt as saying, "You need to stick to your diet." So what should I do?

Tucson, Arizona

How about suggesting the two of you go to Weight Watchers? They're available in almost every major city in the nation and offer a sensible and affordable weight-loss program.

By offering to go *with* her, she's less likely to feel defensive or embarrassed. She'll also know you really care about helping her become the very best she can be.

If she really doesn't want to attend, then suggest that *you're* wanting to get in better shape, and ask her to join you in a regular workout. This could be done three times a week, and the two of you can create it yourselves. For example: On Mondays we'll walk two miles. On Wednesdays we'll ride bikes. On Fridays we'll exercise with an aerobics video.

Above all else, be encouraging. She probably feels bad about gaining weight and right now needs your friendship more than anything. Please don't pressure her. If she really doesn't want to make an effort to lose weight, quit bringing it up. Love her exactly the way she is!

Dear Susie:
There's a boy at my church who wants to be a girl. He never even hangs around boys. Is there anything my friends and I can do to help him?

Grove, Oklahoma

Chances are something traumatic happened to your friend during childhood. Whatever the reason, it's probably too deep for you and your friends to figure out. The best thing you can do for him is to simply be his friend and pray for him.

Dear Susie:
How can I tell if my friend is anorexic? She's fourteen, weighs 105 pounds, and is very pretty. She wants to lose ten pounds. Her diet consists of eating only one meal per day—dinner. Is this a sign of anorexia?

De Motte, Indiana

I think it's too early to tell. It's normal for weight to fluctuate during the teen years because the body is going through so many changes. Though it's not healthy for your friend to limit herself to only one meal a day, it's not automatically a sign of anorexia.

Anorexia is self-starvation. Many girls who fear gaining weight develop anorexia. They lose so much weight that they eventually not only mess up the *outside* of their body but the *inside* as well. For example, most anorexics lose their periods and sometimes lose the chance to give birth. They often lose so much weight that their bodies develop a light "peach fuzz" as a protective device for insulation.

Other signs are obsessive exercise, eating little or nothing, constant obsession with calories and food, and withdrawal.

You might want to check out some books on eating disorders from your local library. As you gain more information, keep an eye on your friend. If you think she's in danger, don't hesitate to speak with an adult.

Dear Susie:

I just found out that one of my church friends is not a virgin. She also cusses, smokes, and does drugs. On top of that, she watches bad movies and listens to sexually explicit songs from rock groups. When her mom found out about all this, she only grounded her, then sent her to a psychiatrist. How can I help her?

Alexandria, Virginia

Make it your goal to live a consistent Christlike life in front of her. Keep loving her and praying for her. I hope she'll see the difference in *your* life and eventually want what you have.

It may take a while though—especially if her parents aren't going to be more assertive in encouraging her to give up that part of her lifestyle. It's also possible that God may want to use you simply to plant a seed in her life and bring someone else along her path later to water it and cause growth.

If she ever brags about her wild lifestyle to you, don't laugh or condone it in any way. Let her talk and always be willing to listen, but make it clear you don't want to have anything to do with those habits.

Dear Susie:

I'm really concerned about my best friend. When her boyfriend gets mad, he and his friends call her "slut"— which is not true about her. She cries all the time but puts up with it.

Waco, Texas

I'm guessing that she puts up with this because she has a low self-esteem. She either believes she doesn't deserve anyone better than the jerk she's with now, or she thinks if she breaks up with him she won't be able to get another boyfriend.

SAD! She needs to be loved—but with genuine, no-strings-attached love. Her boyfriend is "loving" her selfishly. When she doesn't do what he wants, he gets mad. It's obvious that she's in an unhealthy relationship, but what can *you* do?

Affirm her as much as you can about the traits she has that you admire. This will help build her confidence and make her feel better about herself. Also, remind her that you care about her—*really* care—and that you want to see her treated with the respect she deserves.

I also encourage you to get an adult involved—someone she likes and respects. Is there a teacher you both like who would make the time to talk with you? Or your youth leader? Or even your parents? She needs to hear an adult say, "You are valuable, and I don't like what I see and hear from your boyfriend. You deserve much better."

Dear Susie:
My friend, who's twelve, is dating a twenty-year-old. She got mad at me when I told her she's too young for him. How can I help her see the truth?

Chesterfield, South Carolina

Yikes! A twenty-year-old? A couple of questions pop into my head, and I wish we were talking in person instead of through paper so we could really talk this out.

First, do her parents know? Is this out in the open, or is she sneaking around behind their backs to meet this guy?

Second, are you sure they're dating in the true sense of the word? What a twelve-year-old considers to be "dating" is often very different from what a twenty-year-old would label it. Could she be exaggerating what's happening?

Perhaps this twenty-year-old guy is simply being nice to her—saying hi, showing an interest in her schoolwork or activities. She may be interpreting this as dating when it's really not.

And third, why would a twenty-year-old be interested in a twelve-year-old? That's what makes me question her interpretation of "dating." She may *want* you and the rest of her friends to think she's involved in a relationship...but before you do, seek out the facts.

After you have answered the above questions, you'll have a clearer picture of what's really going on. And if she really *is* dating this guy, talk with an adult about helping her see that he really is too old for her. She probably has ZERO dating experience, while he has plenty. This also means that the relationship could easily escalate much farther *physically* than it should.

Bottom line: He's dating a minor!

Dear Susie:
I go to a really small school. We only have fifty students in K–8th grades. There are about fifteen students in my

particular class. I only have one really good friend. The others are just "okay" ones. Any suggestions on how I can make more friends?

Knox, Nebraska

Your disadvantage (being in a small school) can also be your advantage. Think about it: You can get to know everyone in your entire school well! But to *have* friends, you have to *be* a friend. So strive to become the kind of friend to others that you wish they'd be to you. How? Start by making a list of everything you want in a friend. Kindness? Honesty? Sense of humor? High moral standards? Take your time on this—you want to be as thorough and complete as possible.

Next, start at the top of the list and begin fulfilling those qualities with those around you, even though you may not know them well. Make yourself say hi to everyone you pass in the hallway, calling students by name. (Remember, your school is small enough that you can actually DO this!) If you don't know someone's name, find out.

It may seem hard to do this—especially if you don't have an outgoing personality—but remember, this is your heart's desire . . . to make and have more friends. So, if it's not easy, you may have to *make* yourself do this. To see what contemporary Christian artist Margaret Becker did to make friends, see page 67.

Dear Susie:

One of my friends is a shoplifter. She's thirteen years old and started taking things with another friend from school. I have told her not to do it around me, but just the other day she got something worth about twelve dollars when we were together.

She says she doesn't really even *want* to shoplift—she just *does* it. I don't want her to get into trouble, and she's

begging me not to tell anyone. What should I do?

West Chester, Ohio

Time for tough love. Remind her that what she's doing is against the law. Let her know you value her friendship, but not to the extent of either one of you getting into serious trouble. The love chapter (1 Cor. 13) tells us: "If you love someone you will . . . always expect the best of him" (v. 7).

Challenge her to live above the temptation of stealing, and tell her you expect the best of her. Tough love, remember? Tell her you'll go with her to return the merchandise she stole while with you the other day. If she refuses, talk with her parents.

Dear Susie:

My friend thinks a girl can dress any way she wants and boys should still respect her. *I* think that if a girl dresses immodestly she should expect to be treated without respect.

What do *you* think?

Cherokee, North Carolina

A girl can—to a certain extent—set the tone for the entire date just by the way she dresses. I wish girls would consider more carefully *how* they dress. I don't think they realize how powerful what they're wearing can be.

One of the major differences between guys and girls is that guys are visually stimulated, while girls are emotionally stimulated. In other words, it doesn't take much for a guy to become sexually aroused. Many times all it takes is seeing something provocative. Girls need romance and attention.

So are all guys just one big walking hormone? Of course not. Guys who are *gentlemen* (and who let God

140

guide their minds) know how to control themselves. But why make it more difficult for them?

One of the biggest complaints of Christian guys who want to establish godly dating relationships is that many times the girls don't do a lot to help. Guys (full of character) want to date Christian girls who dress fashionably and take time to make themselves look good—but who also dress modestly.

If your friend is dressing provocatively, she can expect guys to think she wants to be "handled." And if she resists when they make physical advances, she'll be known as a "tease." Neither reputation is the greatest, huh?

Play it smart and THINK about what kind of message you're sending by the clothes you wear.

Dear Susie:

Do you think it's okay for an older girl to date a younger guy?

Clearwater, Florida

How much younger? And what's the breakdown? I mean, are we talking about a high school senior dating a sophomore? Or a sophomore dating an eighth grader? Or a junior dating a seventh grader?

The older you get (like in college and after), it doesn't seem to matter as much. When a twenty-two-year-old girl dates a nineteen-year-old guy, there's really not much difference. Nor is there much of a gap when a twenty-seven-year-old dates a twenty-one-year-old. But there *is* a big difference in junior high and high school. You're still in the middle of the developing process— emotionally *and* physically.

I don't see a problem with a couple of years . . . but I would question anything more than that.

Dear Susie:

I'm thirteen years old and have liked this guy at my church since I was eight. Everyone says it's only "puppy love," but I don't think so. What do *you* think?

Burrows, Indiana

Time will tell. If you still feel as strongly at age nineteen as you do now, it's not "puppy love." But maybe the more important question is, How is he responding to you? You can like him forever and ever, but if he doesn't like you back, set your sights on someone else.

DIDJA KNOW
it's not 2 early 2 begin dropping hints about **whatcha want 4** Valentine's Day, Christmas, or your B-day? Here R **my suggestions:**

1. *Getting Ready for the Guy/Girl Thing* by Greg Johnson and Susie Shellenberger. (Simple stuff. Solid stuff. Stuff you GOT 2 know about what the opposite sex is thinking and feeling and why!)
2. A subscription to *Brio* magazine. Hey! It's only fifteen dollars for a whole year. Where else U gonna get the straight scoop on the hottest, the latest, and the best? Stuff on Christians you wanna know more about: Amy Grant, MWS, Steven Curtis Chapman, Candace Cameron, Darius McCrary, Michael Chang, Miss America, Kirk Cameron, DC Talk, Carman, and yep, MORE GUYS!
3. Another copy of *this* book so you can give it 2 your best friend.
4. *Keeping Your Cool While Sharing Your Faith* by Greg Johnson and Susie Shellenberger. Great stuff on sharing your Best Friend with those who don't know him.
5. *Life, Sex and Everything in Between* by Bill Sanders.
6. A collection of Mother Goose nursery rhymes. (*Yeah, I know it's stupid. I want U 2 like the first 5 suggestions the most!*)

11

TOO FAR?

Dear Susie:
I'm fourteen years old and have had at least ten boyfriends in the past six months. But *now* I've finally found the one I want to be with for a long time. He's sixteen and wants to have sex. So do I.

I know it's wrong, but I really want to. I also know you're probably going to tell me not to, but I'm going to anyway—probably in the next two weeks.

We've come very close two other times, but he didn't have a condom on both occasions. We're both virgins and not ready to be parents yet. So I wanted to ask you what other things I can use besides condoms so I'll be prepared for sex with him just in case there are other times when he has no protection.

Los Angeles, California

You're being *lustful,* not *loving. Lust* says, "I want it now!" *Love* says, "I'll wait for you, because you're worth waiting for."

Know what? It all comes down to personal choices. And the choices you make *now* equal consequences *later.*

You're fourteen years old, so it stands to reason that you probably won't marry this young man. You said your-

145

self that you've already had ten different boyfriends. Sounds like you're having trouble understanding what love is. So why are you so anxious to give away a part of yourself to someone you *won't* be spending the rest of your life with?

Because you're lustful. You want what feels good *now*—regardless of the consequences.

Okay, let's say (against all odds) that you *do* stick with this guy throughout the next several years and end up marrying him. By having sex with him now, you're still messing up the trust factor. If he's willing to go against God's law *before* marriage, who's to say he won't do that *after* marriage?

You wrote asking for information on birth control. I don't believe that's what you really want. If so, you wouldn't have written *me*. You also stated you knew what I'd say. Sounds like you really want someone to tell you *not* to have sex. If you simply wanted birth control info, you could check the phone book, a local health clinic, or even a school counselor.

Instead, you chose to write a *Christian* whom you know is going to give you a solid biblical response. So here it is: It's against God's will for you to have sex before marriage. Plain and simple.

Know what I'd love to do? Go play a game of mini-golf with you and chat about why you've had ten different boyfriends, why you skip from one guy to another, and why you're now ready to toss away one of the most important gifts you have (your virginity).

And after you'd smeared me at mini-golf, I'd treat you to a cherry Slurpee, give you a big bear hug, and tell you how special and loved you really are.

Dear Susie:
I made a horrible mistake when I was fourteen years old. I gave up the most precious thing I had—my virginity.

I thought this guy loved me—*really* loved me. So in an emotional moment, I gave it all up for ten minutes of pleasure—or what was *supposed* to be pleasure. You see, it really *wasn't* pleasurable. Afterward, I felt guilty and frightened. I was ashamed.

Not only did I give up my virginity, but I gave up a couple of other things too—my self-respect and my terrific relationship with God. He's done *so much* for me, and by breaking out of his will for my life, I hurt him deeply.

I can't act like he doesn't care or pretend that it doesn't matter. It does. It matters so much he wrote about it in the Ten Commandments. If it wasn't that important, he wouldn't have told us to wait until marriage.

147

I have sought his forgiveness, and I know he's answered my prayers, but it sure has taken a long time for me to *believe* that he still loves me. You can't imagine the battles I've fought in my heart.

For all those girls who say their boyfriend will leave if they don't have sex with them, who cares? Anyone who puts that much pressure on someone isn't worth it.

And for the old argument, "But he *loves* me . . . ," I say that's just baloney with cheese. My advice is, "Please respect *yourself* enough—as well as your relationship with Christ—to say NO!"

I've asked God to wipe my slate clean, and I've made my own personal covenant with him to save myself from now on until marriage. I want to encourage other girls to do the same.

Fremont, California

Thanks for sharing your story with me. You're right; God has wiped your slate completely clean. Isn't it exciting to serve a God who not only forgives but *forgets?* I'm sure your letter will make an impact on others who are in the middle of some heavy questions regarding sexual involvement.

Dear Susie:

My friend lets her boyfriend "feel her up" in the middle of class and in the halls. I'm embarrassed and worried for her. What can I do?

Houlton, Maine

I understand your concern for her. If she's allowing *this* to happen in public, I can't help but wonder what's going on in private! Well . . . that's the problem. Obviously, more *is* going on in private or your friend wouldn't feel so free to act out her sexual escapades in public.

Would you feel comfortable expressing your concern privately to a school counselor? Perhaps a female counselor could help her understand that not only is this not appropriate public behavior, but she's headed for trouble (pregnancy, sexually transmitted diseases, and guilt) if she continues in this manner.

More importantly, though, is the fact that your friend is selling herself short. By putting our sexual desires on hold until marriage, we're setting ourselves up to enjoy God's ultimate best! By becoming too involved *before* marriage (and I'm not just talking about intercourse), we're working toward diminishing his perfect gift for us.

Ask your pastor or youth leader to organize a special series on sex and dating. There are almost zillions of fantastic Christian videos, books, and programs—all geared to teens—on this subject in any Christian bookstore. Would he or she consider using it for your youth group? If so, this would be a terrific thing to plug your friend into.

Don't give up hope! Keep praying for her. Don't preach at her, but let her know where you stand and what you believe about what's going on.

Dear Susie:

I want to wait until I'm married to have sex, but I'm not sure I can. I have a stubborn personality, and I get bored easily.

I'm twelve years old and am so scared of my feelings that I have never even held hands with a boy. Most of my friends have started kissing. It's not that I don't want to; I just don't want to go too far. Help!

Leitchfield, Kentucky

Though holding hands is a long way from having sex, I admire your desire to wait until marriage. But you know what? This has to be *so much more* than just a desire. This has to be a deep commitment you make with God.

If you're going simply on a desire to wait, you probably won't make it till marriage. If your decision is woven into your relationship with Christ, though, *his strength* can pull you through. He's promised that there will be *no* temptation you face that's too great not to be overcome with his power.

Are you familiar with the Love Pendant? It's a beautiful necklace with three question marks and a heart next to each. A diamond is embedded in the middle of the pendant. The three questions stand for personal commitments: Will you save yourself for marriage by being true to yourself, your God, and your future mate?

The Love Pendant is available through Josh McDowell Ministries (P.O. Box 1000, Dallas, TX 75221) and sells for approximately twenty dollars. Will you consider sharing your desire to wait until marriage with your parents? Let them know how serious you are, and ask them to consider getting you this special pendant. Explain to them that you want to be held accountable to God *and* to them for sexual purity.

Tell them it would mean *so much* for them to give you the pendant on a special night—just the three of you—when you can talk about their expectations for you in dating and in establishing godly relationships.

Then, wear the pendant as a reminder of your commitment to God, your family, and yourself.

Dear Susie:

Last Friday I went to our school's football game. After it was over I was saying good-bye to a guy friend. He gave me a big hug, then swung me around. When he finally let me down, his hand slid down from my back to my rear.

I don't want to sound sick or anything, but this really didn't bother me. We stayed like this for about five minutes. All I could think was, "Am I sinning? Is there something wrong with this?" Please help!

Logan, North Dakota

God placed a desire for intimacy and physical contact in each of us. But it's only right to fulfill that in the right context. You were involved in a form of petting, which is caressing a person toward sexual arousal.

"Is this wrong?" you ask. Well, take a look at what the Bible says in 1 Corinthians 7:1: "It is good for a man not to touch a woman" (KJV).

Did the apostle Paul mean that literally? I don't think this wise man of God was talking about patting someone on the back, shaking hands, or even holding hands. I like to think he's saying, "Watch out! Touching to arouse someone sexually is wrong outside of marriage. Why? Because it's like playing with fire! Eventually, you won't be satisfied with that any longer and will end up going too far (having sex) and regretting it."

Though you didn't initiate what happened Friday night, I *am* concerned that you begin *right now* to establish some guidelines for your dating behavior. Who can help you do this? Parents, youth pastor, or a Christian adult friend whom you trust.

I don't want you to get a reputation as being "easy." Friday night you were easy—not because you planned to be—

151

but simply because the unexpected happened and you didn't do anything about it . . . probably because you were shocked, and probably because you didn't know *what* to do.

You've stated that this guy is simply a friend, meaning you haven't even dated him yet. Where does he get off "feeling" a good friend? That's totally inappropriate—and I hope you'll let him know that.

Next time a guy tries the same thing, put a quick stop to it. Remember—you're not helpless! Most guys will go as far as you will let them. So take control!

Dear Susie:

I've just started the ninth grade and already feel like my head's about to explode! I've been looking forward to being in high school for a long time, but I feel like I'm right in the middle of a ton of complicated situations—mostly stuff about guys.

My pastor says we're here to glorify God, and I believe that. But a teenager's a teenager, right? Does glorifying God mean not checking out guys' looks or kissing?

I *know* that I'm not going to have sex until I'm married. I've already made that promise to myself and to God, and I'm determined not to break it. But is there a line that doesn't cross over to sex but *is* crossing too far?

New Orleans, Louisiana

When the Bible was written, teens weren't considered teens. When a guy reached marrying age (puberty), he was tagged as an adult. His parents chose a girl for him to marry, and he did. Dating didn't exist. He didn't have to worry about whether to kiss the girl good night or not. They just got married and didn't have to decide whether or not to have premarital sex.

He had *other* problems . . . like the temptation of prostitutes. But the point is, he had different problems than the ones you face. And kids thirty years from now will encounter different struggles than you have today.

So the Bible isn't specific on "the line" you're asking about. The Word of God never says, "Don't go past a kiss." I know several teens who live with the attitude, "How far can I go without going all the way?" Or "How much can I get away with and still make it into heaven?"

This isn't what Jesus taught his disciples. The question *all* of us should be asking is, "How can I live closer to God?" When the Bible talks about sex, it often refers to "knowing" another person. "Knowing," in this context, means on an intimate level. You can be physically intimate with a guy and not have intercourse. So is everything okay as long as you don't go all the way?

Nope. Based on God's Word, I don't believe this is how he wants you to live your life. You're right about being a teenager. Your sexuality is just now coming alive. You're experiencing some exciting desires and feelings. None of that is wrong. It's how God created you. But it's how you handle it that becomes right or wrong.

I suggest you talk out your questions with an adult. Since your pastor has already mentioned some of the things you're thinking about, how about following up with him? If you're uncomfortable with that, consider chatting with your Sunday school teacher, a parent, or another adult friend. Meanwhile? Study the following verses that can help you establish some terrific dating guidelines, okay?

- ☐ Ephesians 5:3
- ☐ Colossians 3:5
- ☐ Hebrews 10:24
- ☐ Hebrews 13:4

Dear Susie:

This is kind of an embarrassing question, but if the guy doesn't have a name or face, is it okay to fantasize about your wedding night and what sex will be like after you're married?

I plan on waiting till marriage, but I'm very curious.

Akron, Ohio

Curiosity is a natural part of life. It's *normal* to be curious about the things we haven't experienced. I've always wanted to ride in a hot-air balloon, so I'm curious. I think about it, wonder about it, sometimes try to imagine what it would feel like to float through the air, but I don't obsess on it.

It works the same way with sex. You've never had sex, so naturally you're curious about it. It's normal to wonder what it will be like. You can't help what pops into your mind—but you *can* control how long it stays there. When you think about something too much, it becomes an obsession.

Strive to fill your mind with things that won't leave you frustrated or wanting what you can't have. Here's what the Bible says: "Fix your thoughts on what is true and good and right. Think about things that are pure and lovely, and dwell on the fine, good things in others. Think about all you can praise God for and be glad about" (Phil. 4:8).

Dear Susie:

I know you're going to say that it's wrong to do anything—like petting—before marriage, but I'm going to tell you how I feel anyway.

I'm not talking about having sex, just a lot of touching and petting. You're probably going to tell me that petting will lead to intercourse. I KNOW THAT!

See, I've known this guy for a LONG time. We started going out about a month ago. We have done some things

154

that you would consider wrong, but I don't think it is, and I don't feel a bit guilty about it.

I don't think it will lead to us having sex, because I'm not ready until I'm married. He doesn't pressure me at all and says he respects me for not wanting to have sex.

So my question is, what if—because of my own values and beliefs—I don't think it's wrong? And don't tell me to get out of the relationship because I don't want to, and I won't.

Essex, Vermont

Petting isn't just an expression of love *period.* It's an expression of love that has a natural lead-in to something much greater and more powerful. Stopping in between is difficult—and if you're honest—is probably something you really don't *want* to do . . . your body and mind *want* to go further.

I realize that heavy petting is not the same as intercourse, but there are some similarities: no part of the body is off-limits, extreme physical intimacy, getting to really *know* the other person's body and how it responds.

Like it or not, these are the very things God wants reserved for marriage. You say you don't feel it's wrong. But feelings are so undependable, so up and down, so fleeting. Why trust how you *feel* with something as BIG and as IMPORTANT and as LIFE-AFFECTING as sex?

Instead, I encourage you to trust God's Word.

Dear Susie:

I have funny feelings when I'm around girls. Does this mean I'm gay? I don't want to have a "relationship" with a girl; I want to marry a man and have a happy life. Am I bisexual? How can I tell?

Monroe, Wisconsin

You're caught in the middle of puberty right now, which means that your body is going through the process

155

of growing up. This is a time of sexual awakening for you. And *that* means that all kinds of crazy feelings are racing around inside. You're thinking about sex more, and you're experiencing some feelings you've never had before.

None of this makes someone a homosexual. In his book *Preparing for Adolescence,* Dr. James Dobson describes this growing up process: "New chemicals in your body will begin to develop a brand-new appetite when you're between 12 and 15. This will not be a craving for food, but it will involve the matter called sex."

God created us to be attracted to the opposite sex. I don't believe *anyone* is preprogrammed before birth to be a homosexual. I believe it's a choice of behavior that

usually reflects something bigger and deeper going on inside the person's life.

The Bible is clear in stating that practicing homosexuality (being physically involved with someone of the same sex) is a sin. God destroyed Sodom and Gomorrah because of sexual sin—much of it being homosexuality. Though I don't know you, I don't think you're a homosexual or bisexual. I think you're a normal teen girl experiencing the crazy, mixed-up feelings of going through puberty.

If, however, you seriously think you're struggling with some deeper issues related to homosexuality, I encourage you to talk with a professional Christian counselor.

Dear Susie:
Does Amy Grant condone premarital sex?

Puyallup, Washington

No, she doesn't. You can read her story, *Amy Grant, A Biography,* by Bob Millard. She makes some strong statements about premarital sex. You may be familiar with her album *The Loft,* which came about because she and her husband Gary Chapman decided to open their barn loft to teens in the Nashville area.

It started as a weekly event resembling an exciting youth rally filled with singing, skits, and testimonies. Amy and Gary weren't alone in this venture; they had a lot of help from various other Christian artists.

Besides just singing and having a good time, though, the leaders delivered some challenging devotional messages. One of those messages was on sex. They shared from God's Word—as well as from their hearts—the importance of saving your virginity until marriage.

Amy Grant isn't the only one in the spotlight who encourages teens to wait for marriage. Here are a few other personalities you might recognize.

Candace Cameron (Actress, *Full House*): "Since sex is such a unique gift, I don't want to share it with a bunch of people. This is something I want to experience with one person and one person only. So I'm waiting till marriage. I realize not many people share my belief. That's okay."

Toby McKeehan (Musician, DC Talk): "Each of us in DC Talk has chosen not to believe the lie of 'safe sex.' Some of our friends, on the other hand, did buy the lie. Now they have miserable lives . . . and aren't able to pursue their dreams."

Darius McCrary (Actor, *Family Matters*): "When you give in, who are you disappointing? Jesus. It's crazy for me—especially with all kinds of fans and stuff, but I have to think about what the Lord would do if he was in my situation; because he *is* in my situation. He's right here with me.

"So I'm saving myself for my future wife because that's what I believe is right. It's a matter of respect—for myself and the person I plan to marry."

David Robinson (Center for the San Antonio Spurs): "Too many people think, Well, I'm not going to abstain from sex, so I'll just try 'safe sex.' But you have a choice to make, and if you make the wrong choice, you're going to have to suffer the consequences. As a Christian, I'm not accepting anything less than God's best."

Chris Castile (Actor, *Step by Step, Beethoven,* and *Beethoven's 2nd*): "I'm definitely keeping myself abstinent until marriage. Everyone is NOT doing it. Look at A. C. Green [Phoenix Suns]—he's not married and he still hasn't done it.

"You think it'll never happen to you—you'll never get diseases—look at what happened to Magic Johnson. I don't want to have to deal with the possibility of AIDS, and I don't want to experience the guilt I'd have. God has a much higher calling on my life—and that is to save this wonderful gift for a lifetime commitment: marriage."

Kirk Cameron (Actor): "It's easy to look at life as a great ride or an awesome game and decide that you're out to have as much fun as you can. And some people see sex that way. But a condom can't protect you from a broken heart. Sex within marriage is the only kind that's truly fun and exciting—the kind that lasts for a lifetime. I'm glad I waited."

Dear Susie:
I'm thirteen years old, and I had sex with my boyfriend two months ago. I've missed my period for two months, and I've gained twelve pounds. I think I'm pregnant. What should I do? And, no, my mom doesn't know.

Tallahassee, Florida

Though it will be superhard, you *have* to tell your mom. She'll find out eventually anyway, so the sooner, the better. And she needs to hear it from *you*—not your friends, your boyfriend, or a doctor.

Yes, there's a good chance you're pregnant. At least it sounds that way! After you talk with your mom, the two of you will want to make an appointment with a gynecologist who can determine for sure if you're pregnant and how far along you are.

If you *are* pregnant, I beg you to give this little life a chance. There are thousands of couples across the nation desperately wanting to adopt. Please don't even consider abortion as an option. Two wrongs never make a right.

Also, know there's absolutely NOTHING you can do to make God stop loving you. Though it *is* a sin to have sex outside of marriage, you serve a God who wants to give you a brand-new start.

Seek God's forgiveness, then establish some dating accountability with your parents, youth pastor, or close friends—people who know you and can help you set healthy physical limits with those you date.

HERE'S A QUARTER. CALL MY DAD. TELL HIM WHAT YOU WANT TO DO. IF IT'S ALL RIGHT WITH HIM, IT'S OKAY WITH ME.

LOVER'S LANE

Dear Susie:

My new boyfriend and I are both Christians. A couple of days ago, he asked me if I wanted to have sex. I told him no and explained that I wanted to save myself for marriage.

We both agreed that I was right. Is there a chance that since I declined, he'll respect me for it and never ask me that question again?

Clarion County, Pennsylvania

Yes, there's a chance. But since he asked you once, chances are—in the heat of the moment—he'll probably ask you again. My advice? Try to avoid heated moments. For instance, refuse to be alone together in an empty house. Too much temptation. Why set yourselves up?

Try to involve yourselves in more group dating situations, do more things in public (bowling, mini-golf, shopping), and verbally agree *before you go out again* what your limits are.

Dear Susie:

I'm sixteen years old and have read your column in *Brio* magazine. Since so many girls write to you about premarital sex, I wanted to share my own experience.

A year ago I met a guy whom I thought was the one I'd stay with for a long time. He made me feel really special. After about seven months of being together, we had sex. Because I believed I loved him, I rationalized it was okay. Now I'm pregnant. I've lost my friends (yeah, they still care, but they have their own lives, you know?), my school activities (how can you play on the volleyball team when you're pregnant?), the father of the baby (he's with someone else now), my freedom, and the most valuable gift I had—my virginity.

I hate the wall I've put between God and me . . . and am working hard at getting back to the great relationship we once had. I'm also having to reestablish trust within my family.

Any guy who says he loves you *will wait* if he REALLY loves you! The pain you experience from having sex before marriage is not worth a moment of fun.

I will raise this baby to know Jesus Christ, and hopefully I can teach him/her not to make the same mistake I did. For anyone who's considering having sex with her boyfriend, let me encourage you to ask, "What would Jesus do?" That settles it, doesn't it?

Elko, Nevada

Wow. I'm impressed with your openness, your sincerity, and your willingness to share yourself with others who need your insight. Thank you for your honesty.

Dear Susie:

I'm starting to like a guy at school. I don't think he's a Christian, and I don't know him too well. I'd like to be his friend before anything else. How can I get to know him better without dating him?

Birmingham, Alabama

I admire the fact that you want to be his friend *first*. You're thinking about an important aspect that many girls overlook. How do you become friends with *anyone?* Talk with him, invite him to church activities, show an interest in his hobbies.

One question you need to be aware of though, is What happens after friendship? Well, maybe just a stronger friendship. And that's good. But what if you *both* start to like each other more than friends?

Please establish your dating standards *now*—ahead of time—so you'll know what you believe and why. And how do you do this? Parents, youth leaders, and adults whom you have a lot of confidence in can all help. Most of all, seek God's direction.

Dear Susie:

This guy says he only wants to be friends, but he *treats* me like a girlfriend. He comes over a lot after school. My mom and I both like him.

Eau Claire, Wisconsin

What does "treating you like a girlfriend" mean? If you're interpreting his coming over after school as fact that he wants you to be his girlfriend, I think you're jumping to conclusions. He's already *told* you he just wants a friendship, so don't push him for something more.

The question is: Can you be happy with a friendship? Will you accept that? Or are you going to be constantly trying to turn him into your boyfriend? If so, that's not fair to him. He has stated his intentions. Honor that.

If he's actually doing other things, like holding your hand, bringing you gifts, calling you every day, or trying to kiss you, then you're right—he *is* saying and doing two different things.

Evaluate the relationship as honestly as you can. If he's being nice, coming over to your house, watching TV, and saying he just wants to be friends, then believe him. If, however, he's doing more, then explain your confusion to him.

NOW
that you've
finished . . .

You may disagree, think I'm speaking a foreign language, feel that I'm too conservative, wish I'd write about how to make Rice Krispie treats instead, or write your own book. More than simply pushing my beliefs on you, I hope you will be moved to *react*. Because then you'll stop, think, and establish your own set of beliefs.

Feel free to send me your thoughts, ideas, candy corn, photos, packets of grape Kool-Aid . . . but please don't send leftover cafeteria food, socks with holes, old TV Guides, your parents' electric bill, old shoestrings, or your unfinished homework assignments.

Susie

Susie Shellenberger
Brio
8605 Explorer Drive
Colorado Springs, CO 80920

SUGGESTED READING

Bibles

Life Application Bible for Students (Living Bible). Wheaton: Tyndale, 1988.

Serendipity Bible Study for Groups (NIV). Grand Rapids: Zondervan, 1990.

The Adventure Bible (NIV). Grand Rapids: Zondervan, 1989.

The King and the Beast (Contemporary English Version). Nashville: Nelson, 1991.

The New Student Bible (NIV). Grand Rapids: Zondervan, 1992.

The Transformer (NIV). Nashville: Nelson, 1988.

Youth Study Bible (New Century Version). Loveland, Colo.: Group Publishing, 1987.

Devotions

Burns, Jim. *Getting in Touch with God.* Eugene, Oreg.: Harvest House, 1986.

Christian, S. Rickly. *Alive.* Grand Rapids: Zondervan, 1990.

Christian, S. Rickly. *Alive Two.* Grand Rapids: Zondervan, 1990.

Drescher-Lehman, Sandra. *Just Between God and Me.* Grand Rapids: Zondervan, 1991.

Littleton, Mark. *Beefin' Up.* Portland: Multnomah, 1990.

Littleton, Mark. *Tunin' Up.* Portland: Multnomah, 1992.

Peterson, Lorraine. *Radical Advice from the Ultimate Wiseguy.* Minneapolis: Bethany, 1990.

Shellenberger, Susie. *Soaring Straight Ahead.* Kansas City: Beacon Hill, 1991.

Shellenberger, Susie. *Straight Ahead.* Kansas City: Beacon Hill, 1987.

Stephens, Andrea. *Ready for Prime Time: Devotions for Girls.* Grand Rapids: Baker Book House, 1991.

Tirabassi, Becky. *Live It!* Grand Rapids: Zondervan, 1990.

Worley, Mike. *Brand Name Christians.* Grand Rapids: Zondervan, 1988.

Eating Disorders

Chapian, Marie and Neva Coyle. *Free to Be Thin.* Minneapolis: Bethany House, 1979.

165

O'Neill, Cherry Boone. *Starving for Attention*. New York: Dell, 1983.

Rowland, Cynthia, *The Monster Within*. Grand Rapids: Baker, 1985.

Bray-Garretson, Helen and Kaye V. Cook. *Chaotic Eating*. Grand Rapids: Zondervan, 1992.

The following are available from Focus on the Family (1-800-232-6459):

- "Escaping Anorexia and Bulimia" (free booklet LF 197)
- "Eating Right: A Guide to Family Nutrition" (free booklet LF 125)
- "Eating Disorders" (two-part cassette CS078, five dollars)
- "When Food Is an Enemy" (cassette CS304, five dollars)

Sex/Dating

Johnson, Greg, and Susie Shellenberger. *Getting Ready for the Guy/Girl Thing*. Ventura, Calif.: Regal, 1991.

Johnson, Greg, and Susie Shellenberger. *What Hollywood Won't Tell You about Love, Sex, and Dating*. Ventura, Calif.: Regal, 1994.

McDowell, Josh, and Dick Day. *Why Wait?* San Bernardino, Calif.: Here's Life Publishers, 1987.

Sanders, Bill. *Life, Sex and Everything in Between*. Grand Rapids: Revell, 1991.

Youth Group

Rydberg, Denny. *Creative Bible Studies for Young Adults*. Loveland, Colo.: Group Publishing, 1990.

Leonard, Larry, and Jack McCormick. *Youth Program Hour Idea Book*. Kansas City: Beacon Hill, 1985.

Rice, Wayne. *Great Ideas for Small Youth Groups*. Grand Rapids: Zondervan, 1986.

Yaconelli, Mike and Scott Koenigsaecker. *Get 'Em Talking*. Grand Rapids: Zondervan, 1989.

Other

Brio magazine. Call 1-800-A-FAMILY for a free sample copy.

Baker, Pat. *Dear Diary . . . The Secret Feelings of a Junior High Girl*. Wheaton: Tyndale, 1990.

Dobson, James. *Preparing for Adolescence*. New York: Bantam, 1984.

Millard, Bob. *Amy Grant, A Biography*. New York: Doubleday, 1986.

Shellenberger, Susie, and Greg Johnson. *Keeping Your Cool While Sharing Your Faith*. Wheaton: Tyndale, 1993.

INDEX

Index